Dane

Ayrshire Coast

Skelmorlie to Glen App

Fort Publishing Ltd

Acknowledgements

The author would like to thank all those people who explored the Ayrshire coast in his company, introducing him to a wonderful piece of Scottish countryside.

First published in 2001 by Fort Publishing Ltd, Old Belmont House, 12 Robsland Avenue, Ayr, KA7 2RW.

Maps reproduced by permission of Ordnance Survey on behalf of the Controller of Her Majesty's Stationery Office © Crown Copyright. MC 100034421.

Cover design by Paul McLaughlin, 48 Queen Street, Lochmaben, Dumfries, DG11 1PS

Printed in Great Britain by Bell and Bain Ltd, Glasgow.

ISBN 0-9536576-4-7

A catalogue record for this book is available from the British Library

Contents

Introduction   5
    Access   7
    Ordnance Survey Maps   7
    Accommodation   8
    Transport   9
    Outline Map   10
Skelmorlie   11
Skelmorlie Castle   13
Meigle Bay and Beyond   14
Knock Castle   16
Routenburn Road   17
Largs   20
Kelburn Castle   29
Fairlie   30
Hunterston   34
Hunterston Power Station   37
Hunterston Castle and House   38
The Portencross Murder   39
The Hunterston Brooch   40
Portencross   41
Portencross Castle   42
Seamill   44
Ardrossan-North Bay   46
Horse Isle   47
Ardrossan   48
Ardrossan Castle   49
Saltcoats   52
Ardeer to Irvine   55
Irvine   56
Gailes   63
Barassie   65
Troon   66
Prestwick-St Andrew's House   71
Prestwick   72
Maryborough and Bentfield   75
Newton upon Ayr   77
Ayr   78
Doonfoot   86

Contents

Greenan Castle	88
Fisherton	91
Dunure	92
Dunure Castle	95
Croy	97
Culzean Castle	100
Maidens	105
Turnberry	107
Dipple	111
The Curragh to Girvan Mains	112
Newton Kennedy	113
Girvan	114
Ailsa Craig	117
Ardmillan	120
Kennedy's Pass	122
Shipwreck Memorial	123
Lendalfoot	124
Carleton Castle	125
Charles Berry's Memorial	126
Sawney Bean's cave	128
Bennane Head	129
Snib's Cairn	130
Ballantrae	131
Ardstinchar Castle	135
Garleffin	136
Glenapp Hills	137
Glen App	139
Postman's Memorial	140
Finnarts Bay	141
Bibliography	144

Ayrshire Coast-Introduction

The Ayrshire coast is a place of infinite variety. From the ever-popular seaside resorts in the north, through the more industrialised central stretches and on to the spectacular vistas and picturesque villages in the south, it has something for everyone. There is also its rich history, marked out by the impressive castles and fortified houses; the world-renowned golf courses; the miles of golden sands; the mysterious caves and coves; the colourful cast of characters including William Wallace, Robert the Bruce, Oliver Cromwell, Robert Burns and the legendary cannibal, Sawney Bean.

This book also has the walker or cyclist in mind, and within its pages are explanations of where to walk or cycle. Much of the coast is readily accessible by car, but here and there the

public road has to leave the coast behind for a variety of reasons, be it the terrain, or else because of industrial sites, such as the massive ICI complex at Ardeer.

Those on foot will find that the coastal walk detailed in this book is around 94 miles long. There are many fine walks to enjoy and the scenery is often stunning to behold. Cyclists are also well served. There is an official cycle route for much of the way from Largs to Ayr, and the other stretches have good roads to follow. Happily, the sight of cyclists making their way along the coast is now a familiar one.

5

Ayrshire Coast

The coast is home to some magnificent beaches, where picnickers and paddlers enjoy miles of golden sands in the summer. Other stretches are shingly, but my favourite spots are those places where the rocks have unusual formations and the waves gurgle and rumble in the narrow crevices. Although there are many attractive towns and villages along Ayrshire's coast, there are innumerable spots to get away from it all, and have the place to yourself.

Fisherman sculpture at Irvine

The coastline has a notable heritage, and there is an important range of castles and fortifications from various periods. The Romans are known to have visited Ayrshire's coast, and there are a few traces of them to be found. Bronze Age and Iron Age relics are also few in number, and there is only the odd standing stone or cliff-top fort indicating that they once zealously guarded this coast from the enemy.

It is from the Middle Ages and later that we find the most interesting remains. Who does not marvel at the precarious position of Greenan Castle, with its tales of murder and clan feuding? Or at Portencross Castle and its associations with the ancient kings of Scotland? The best known castle is undoubtedly Culzean which, although rebuilt in its present form in the 18th century by Robert Adam, still has at its core an ancient tower house of the feuding Kennedy family.

More modern conflicts are also well represented, from the old airfield at Turnberry to the gun emplacement at Finnarts Bay, designed to repel the enemy ships and submarines that were expected in the Firth of Clyde, but never came.

Ayrshire is one of Scotland's finest golfing counties, and dotted along the coast are some of the best golf links to be found anywhere in the world. There is the spectacular course at Turnberry, with its distinctive lighthouse and the sea view across the firth to Ailsa Craig. There is also Prestwick Golf Course, where the first British Open was held in 1860, as well as Royal Troon, the scene of many memorable Opens.

The industrial segments of the coast also have much of interest for the visitor. Hunterston Power Station has a first rate visitor centre, and the ICI works at Ardeer are celebrated in the Big Idea exhibition and visitor centre across the footbridge from Irvine harbour.

Access

The routes recommended in this book are not necessarily rights of way, but in most cases are well-walked routes that the public has open access to. If in any doubt about a section of the way, ask locally. The shore between low and high tide levels is in most cases Crown property and no restrictions generally apply to this area.

Ordnance Survey Maps

The maps in this book are for guidance and illustrative purposes only. They are reproduced at a scale of 1:25,000, or approximately 2½ inches to one mile. Those wishing to explore the coastline and its vicinity in greater detail should use the relevant Ordnance Survey maps. Three "Landranger" maps cover the whole Ayrshire coast at a scale of 1:50,000 and provide a detailed layout of the area. The maps are as follows:

Sheet 63, Firth of Clyde, Greenock & Rothesay.
Sheet 70, Ayr, Kilmarnock & Troon.
Sheet 76, Girvan, Ballantrae & Barrhill.

Those folk, like myself, who prefer a more detailed map will find the "Explorer" range more useful. These cover the countryside at a scale of 1:25,000, but the larger number of sheets required means that it is more expensive to collect the five that cover the coast:

Ayrshire Coast

Sheet 309, Stranraer & The Rhins.
Sheet 317, Ballantrae, Barr & Barrhill.
Sheet 326, Ayr & Troon.
Sheet 333, Kilmarnock & Irvine.
Sheet 341, Greenock, Largs & Millport.

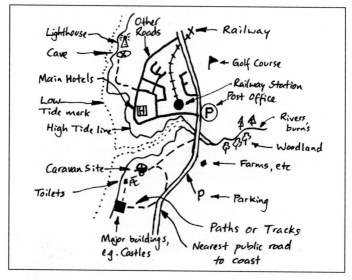

Key Map showing symbols used in main maps.

Accommodation

There is accommodation in all price ranges available over the whole length of the coast, and the only areas where it is limited are those between Ballantrae and Finnarts Bay, and the stretch around Portencross and Hunterston. In all other parts, there is a ready supply of campsites, caravan sites, bed and breakfast establishments and hotels. There is, however, only one youth hostel (at Ayr). It is advisable to book in advance, particularly in the summer months.

*Anchorage
Inn, Dunure*

This can be done privately, or by using one of Ayrshire & Arran Tourist Board's information centres, which can be found at Largs, Irvine, Ayr and Girvan.

Transport

The coast is well served by buses and all the principal roads from Skelmorlie to Ayr have services. Buses are less frequent around Dunure and the Maidens, for the main service is through Maybole to Turnberry and Girvan. The service continues to Stranraer.

The railway network is well developed and many journeys provide excellent views of the coast. The station at Wemyss Bay is ideal for starting a tour from the north, being located a few hundred yards across the border in Renfrewshire. The next station south is at Largs, followed by stations at Fairlie, West Kilbride, Ardrossan, Saltcoats, Stevenston and Kilwinning. This line then heads north to Glasgow. Alternatively the Ayr line can be taken from Kilwinning, travelling south through stations at Irvine, Barassie, Troon, Prestwick Airport, Prestwick Town, Newton-upon-Ayr, and Ayr, before the line heads inland via Maybole station before returning to the coast at Girvan station. The next station to the south of Girvan of any use is Stranraer, 8 miles from the Ayrshire border.

Skelmorlie is the northernmost village in Ayrshire. The village is of relatively recent origin, being feued out from 1850 as a fashionable seaside resort for wealthy businessmen from Glasgow and Renfrewshire. They built desirable houses along the roadside in what is Lower Skelmorlie, the first of these being the Italianate Beach House (1844), almost the first house encountered after crossing the Kelly Water from Renfrewshire into Ayrshire. It is now a nursing home.

Virtually on the border is the old Free Church (1874), now divided into flats. Beyond Beach House is the Parish Church (1895), the work of John Honeyman. By the side of the stairs is a wrought-iron lamp stand, believed to be the work of the celebrated architect and artist, Charles Rennie Mackintosh.

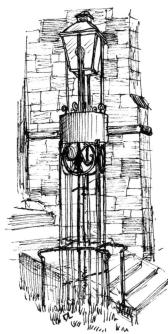

There are a number of hotels along the main road, including Heywood, Albyn and Redcliffe. The architecture of the large houses hereabouts is typically Victorian, including baronial and cottage-ornee styles. In the gardens of some houses are caves in the raised beach cliff-face.

Upper Skelmorlie was built above the conglomerate cliff, away from the constant drum of passing traffic. Here the houses are more spread out, arranged in fine crescents with substantial gardens surrounding them. Skelmorlie Hydro was a large baronial hotel, erected in 1868, with Turkish, salt-water and other baths, but now demolished.

Lampstand at
Skelmorlie Parish Church

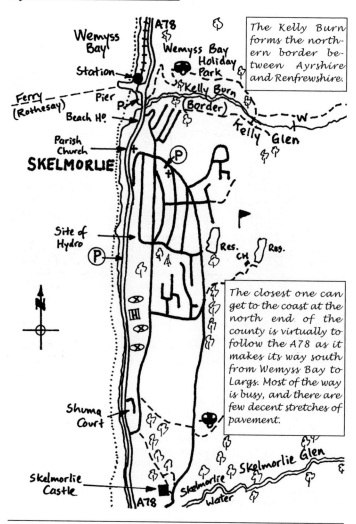

The Kelly Burn forms the northern border between Ayrshire and Renfrewshire.

Wemyss Bay

A78

Wemyss Bay Holiday Park

Station

Kelly Burn (Border)

Ferry (Rothesay)

Pier

Beach Ho.

Kelly Glen

W

Parish Church

SKELMORLIE

P

Site of Hydro

P

Res.   Res.

CH

The closest one can get to the coast at the north end of the county is virtually to follow the A78 as it makes its way south from Wemyss Bay to Largs. Most of the way is busy, and there are few decent stretches of pavement.

N

Shuma Court

Skelmorlie Castle

A78

Skelmorlie Water

Skelmorlie Glen

Visible from the main road is Skelmorlie Castle, rising above the trees. The oldest part of the castle, seat of the Earl of Eglinton and Winton, is said to date from 1502. This is a three-storey tower with corner turrets. An office and a stable range were added in 1636.

Skelmorlie Castle

Later additions were made to the tower in 1850-2, but most of these were demolished following a fire in 1959 and the castle restored to what it may have looked like in the 16th century, making it a more manageable size.

In 1608 Timothy Pont described the building as "a fair veill-built house, and pleasantly seatted, decored with orchards and woodes, the inheritance of Robert Montgomery, Laird thereof." His ancestors received the lands in 1461 (previously being owned by the Cunninghams).

John Graham (c.1795-1886) tenanted the castle for a time. He was a noted collector of art, having made his fortune in the Glasgow textile industry. It was he who extended the castle in the middle of the 19th century.

Ayrshire Coast-Meigle Bay and Beyond

From the southern end of the village of Skelmorlie, one can get no nearer the coast than by following the A78. Shortly after passing a road climbing to Skelmorlie Castle and Mains caravan site the Skelmorlie Water, a short but fast-flowing stream, is traversed. The water joins the firth at Meigle Bay. Parking is available at the south end of the bridge.

Meigle is a hamlet with a few houses arranged around the foot of the stream. In 1876 a small chapel was built of concrete here. Much older is a curved mound of sand, topped with trees, known locally as the Serpent Mound. This may have some connection with early sun worship.

At the south end of the bay is Ashcraig House, located in the trees behind a stone wall.

There are a few cottages located at the road up to Auchengarth, spread out on the hillside above the shore.

At St Fillan's Bridge the Blackhouse Burn is crossed, and on the south side of the bridge a minor road strikes inland. It is possible to return to Meigle Bay this way, or else head south to Largs by a road known locally as the Red Road. Up the short link road is the Manor Park Hotel, distinguished by its squat tower. On the hillside above it is the site of St Fillan's Well. The site of an old chapel associated with this saint was located on the moor here, but there are no remnants of it to be found.

The energetic may fancy an ascent of The Knock, a prominent hill of 712 feet that rises behind Knock Castle. From St Fillan's Bridge a minor road leads to the Red Road, and at the triangular junction a track follows the Blackhouse Burn through the woods and onto the moor. The track continues down to Brisbane Mains, but at the pass a second pathway can be followed in a loop around and up to the summit, which is marked by an Ordnance Survey triangulation station. The views are spectacular, and it is well worth the climb. Here also is a ruined hill fort, the walls of which were timber-laced and vitrified to form a robust defence. This covers an area of 165 feet by 95 feet, and beyond it are further rock-cut ditches and mounds.

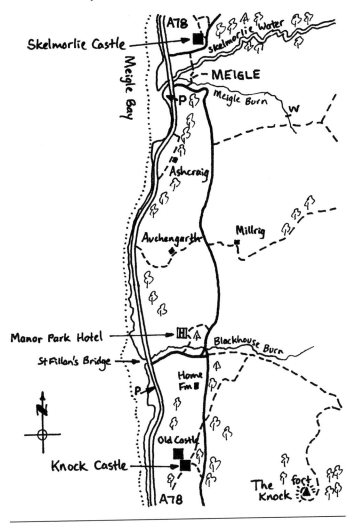

Ayrshire Coast-Knock Castle

There are two Knock Castles here, both perched high above the coast road, looking over the wooded braes and the Firth of Clyde to Cowal and Bute. The old castle dates from 1603-4, and was built with a Z-plan, though half of it has virtually disappeared. The surviving half, which is partially roofed, was rebuilt in 1853 as a form of garden folly for the new castle (becoming the gardener's cottage), hence the walling and turrets.

The Frasers, a branch of the Highland Frasers of Lovat, built Old Knock Castle. They acquired the estate by marrying the heiress around 1400. One of the Frasers was a supporter of Montrose and took part in the Battle of Philiphaugh in 1645. The castle was sold in 1674 to the Montgomeries of Skelmorlie. Since that time it has been owned by many different families.

The new castle was erected in 1853 to the plans of John Thomas Rochead (1814-78), architect of the Wallace Monument at Stirling, and many gothic churches. Knock is a Tudor Gothic structure, dominated by its tower and crenellations. The house was built for Robert Steele, an industrialist from Greenock.

<u>The Knock above Routenburn Road, Largs</u>

From below Knock Castle the A78 continues to follow the coast below Quarter House, which is perched above the raised beach in a similar manner to Knock. Soon the northern fringes of Largs are reached, here spreading linearly along the road. A few large houses have views of the beach and across to the north end of Great Cumbrae, but many are being demolished and newer, high-density flats put in their place.

A bridge crosses the Routen Burn. Routenburn House, which no longer survives, was a school and military hospital in its day.

The main road leaves the waterside for a short distance, heading inland to the bridge over the Noddsdale Water. On the east parapet are two stones stating, "Built 1736 Rebuilt 1824 reconstructed 1977". The reconstruction was a totally new bridge of concrete and Fyfestone.

Distinguished by its tall conical roof is the former gatehouse to Netherhall House, home to Lord Kelvin, as outlined on the plaques. The former archway through which carriages were driven has been glazed and incorporated into the house.

The water has created a delta of land that has been built on. Various private houses and short streets occupy the northern side of the river. However, there is no access to the beach from this side. Immediately on the south side of the bridge a path leads down by the waterside to Auberly Park. This route is more pleasant for cyclists and pedestrians.

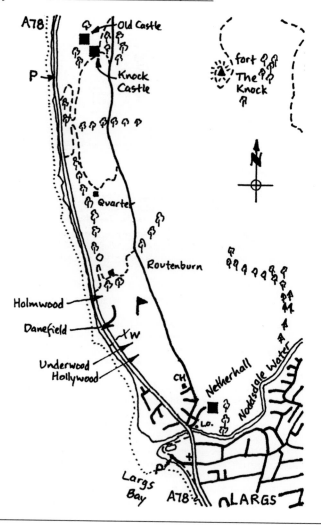

On the north side of the Noddsdale Bridge is the former gatehouse to Netherhall House, bearing a blue plaque to Lord Kelvin. Netherhall itself is now divided into flats. This chateau-like house was erected in 1875 to a design by Campbell Douglas. It cost £12,000 to build, and is said to have been the first house in Scotland to have electric lighting.

The client was Sir William Thomson, Lord Kelvin, the famous Glasgow scientist (1824-1907) who made outstanding discoveries in geomagnetism, electricity, thermodynamics, navigation and other fields. Although born in Belfast, he moved to Glasgow at the age of eight. He was appointed Professor of Mathematics and Natural Philosophy at the age of 22, and in 1848 proposed the Absolute, or Kelvin, temperature scale. Among his many inventions were a tide predictor, siphon recorder and a mirror galvanometer, the last-named being instrumental in creating his wealth.

Thomson was created Baron Kelvin of Largs in 1892 and when he died was honoured by burial in Westminster Abbey, lying beside Sir Isaac Newton.

Another memorial to Kelvin is found within St Columba's Episcopal Church, located at the north end of the promenade.

From the Noddsdale Bridge a path makes its way down the side of the river to its mouth in Largs Bay. The attractive Aubery Park has public conveniences, a boating pond, crazy golf and children's play-park. In the garden is a seagull sculpture from 1963. The park is the northern extremity of Largs Promenade, which can be followed for two miles or so southward to the Pencil.

The first buildings on the left form a slightly curved terrace overlooking the bay and the island of Great Cumbrae. There follows St Columba's Episcopal Church, its entrance doorway located in an unfinished tower, capped by a rather odd pitched roof. St Columba's dates from 1877 and was designed by Ross and MacBeth. The manse is now a private house, its gardens occupied by flats.

The Promenade continues to the RNLI lifeboat station. This was established in 1964 with a D-class boat, but in 1998 the present station was erected and an Atlantic 75-class boat installed. The lifeboat station has a small souvenir outlet and snack bar.

On the landward side of the main road is Vikingar!, the former Barrfields Pavilion (1929). This is a popular visitor centre that tells the story of Largs' Viking connections.

North Promenade

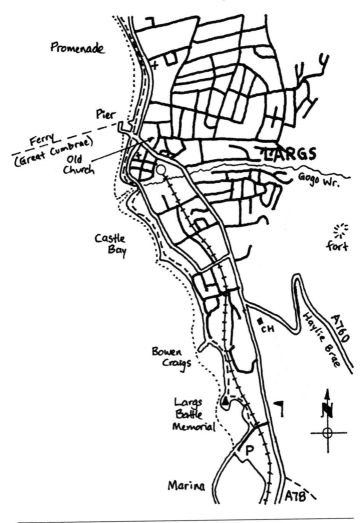

From the lifeboat station the promenade is followed southwards. On the opposite side of the street is the Roman Catholic Church of St Mary, Star of the Sea, a modern building (1962) that has a granite sculpture of Mary and Child, by Hew Lorimer, on the outside. Next to it is Moorburn House (1876), now council offices,

followed by Brooksby House Hospital (David Hamilton, 1837) and Brisbane House Hotel.

At the foot of Nelson Street is Nardini's Café which, with its striking Art Deco interior, is one of the town's most celebrated buildings. The Nardini family's ice cream is renowned throughout Scotland for its exceptional quality. The café was built in 1935 to the plans of Charles Davidson.

The other side of Nelson Street is occupied by the large red sandstone St Columba's Parish Church with its prominent spire housing a clock. The church, which replaced the old parish church, was designed by Henry Steele & Andrew Balfour (1891-3) and contains attractive windows by Cottier & Co., Douglas Strachan, Alfred and Gordon Webster. Within are a war memorial by Sir Robert Lorimer and a memorial to Sir Thomas MakDougall Brisbane. The church is open to the public on weekday mornings.

Soon the amusements are reached, and here can also be found public conveniences and Largs Tourist Information Centre. On the opposite side of the street from the information centre is a small square garden area, in the centre of which is a restored wellhead.

Longboat sculpture

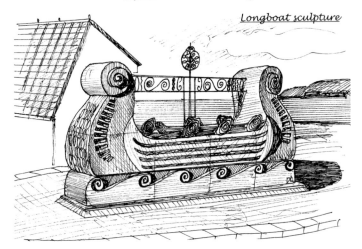

The small harbour at Largs is little more than an L-shaped quay, now mainly used for Caledonian MacBrayne's Cumbrae ferry. From here cars and pedestrians are taken across the short stretch of water (the trip only lasts 10 minutes and takes place every 15 minutes in the summer months) to the island of Great Cumbrae, on which the resort of Millport is located. Although now within the North Ayrshire Council boundary, the Cumbrae islands were originally part of the county of Bute.

The older ferries landed at the slip that survives to the north of the pier. In 1834 the present rubble pier was erected at a cost of £4,275, and here many passenger steamers halted awhile on their trips "Doon the Watter". They were able to tie up on the outside of the pier at any state of the tide.

Near the ferry terminal is a stone and iron sculpture of a Viking longship, unveiled on 20 August 1993 by Stewart Dewar, Convenor of Cunninghame District Council. Across the road rises The Moorings, a block of flats erected in a nautical style in 1987 to the plans of MacMillan & Cronin. This replaced an older building of 1935 by James Houston, which also had a nautical theme.

*The MV "Lochaline"
leaving Largs pier for
Great Cumbrae*

The town of Largs is ancient, and the Romans had a resort here, Roman Baths being unearthed in 1820, "in the garden of Mrs Hall, the local postmistress." A later Bath House of 1816 is located between Bath and Fort streets, adjoining a tea-room. Today, however, Largs is a very popular seaside resort and a douce haven for the retired.

The busy Main Street strikes inland from the pier, heading for the bridge over the Gogo Water. Here can be found the railway and bus stations, as well as numerous shops of all kinds. The railroad was prevented from going any further north by a group of landowners.

Largs was subject to a terrible plague in 1644, and in Noddsdale is an old gravestone commemorating Rev William Smith who died from it in September 1647. He was only 28 years old and had served the parish for just three years. Smith prophesied that the plague would not revisit the town, so long as two holly trees planted at his last resting-place were never allowed to meet.

There are a number of notable antiquities in Largs, including: the ancient Moot Hill of the early town, located in the old churchyard; "Margaret's Law", a burial chamber in Douglas Park; and the Green Hill, above Waterside Street. Above the town, at Cockmalane cottage, is the ancient fort on Castle Hill.

Skelmorlie Aisle

Just off the Main Street, reached through a narrow lane, is the old churchyard of Largs. Here one can find the gable remnants of the original church, as well as a mound of unknown origin. Among the old gravestones there is a cist dating from the Bronze Age and a burial aisle associated with the Brisbanes of that Ilk. This is a simple slab-roofed structure dating from 1634.

More interesting, however, is the highly impressive Skelmorlie Aisle, a burial mausoleum dating from 1636. This was erected for Sir Robert Montgomerie of Skelmorlie Castle and his wife, Margaret Douglas. It is now protected by Historic Scotland, and open to the public (check times at the Information Centre). Externally the building is relatively unadorned, apart from the doorway and the arms above. The large plain arch originally joined the aisle to the parish church, but was demolished in 1802.

On entering the simple stone structure one is totally unprepared for the view. Within is an elaborately carved Renaissance-style tomb, the whole structure being covered with carvings. The original memorial was to have carved effigies of the deceased in the centre, but these were probably never added.

The barrel-vaulted ceiling has a wooden lining, which has been painted with various scenes depicting the seasons, texts from the Geneva Bible, signs of the Zodiac and the arms of the tribes of Israel. This was the work of J Stalker in 1638. It is well worth making a short detour to visit this hidden treasure.

Ayrshire Coast-Largs-Fort Street

From Largs Pier one can walk south along the promenade to the mouth of the Gogo Water. The route commences at Fort Street, which leads past the former Bath House of 1816, now the Brisbane Centre. Behind it can be seen the tall spire of the sandstone Clark Memorial Church (William Kerr of T.G. Abercrombie, 1890-2), which is opened by arrangement. John Clark of the Paisley thread-making firm, Anchor, gifted it to the town. Built in the early English Gothic style, the church has a hammer beam roof, windows by Stephen Adam, Meikle & Sons, and C.W. Whall, and a fine peel of bells in the steeple. On the gable of the church are carvings of Moses and St John.

Next door to the Clark church is the Romanesque St John's Parish Church, dating from 1886 (A.J. Graham) when it was built as a Free Church. Constructed of blonde sandstone, the tower is dwarfed by that of its neighbour.

On the lawn in front of the sandstone block known as Sandringham is the burgh war memorial. The route has to be taken inland for a short stretch to the Brisbane Bridge. This was erected in 1911 and commemorates Sir Thomas MakDougall Brisbane, already mentioned. He was also a noted astronomer, and pillars in this part of the town were associated with— his observatory.

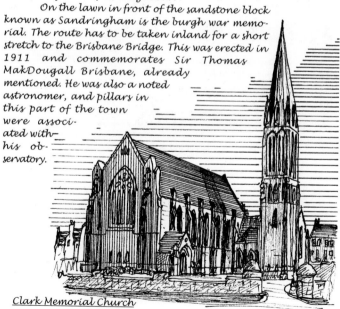

Clark Memorial Church

On the south side of the Gogo Water is located the Broomfields part of the town, the park presented to Largs by Sir Thomas MakDougall Brisbane. The coast is less developed here, and pathways can be followed around Castle Bay towards Cairnies Quay.

On the seaward side of the street is another open stretch of grass, in the midst of which is a disused granite fountain commemorating Dr Campbell, for 61 years physician to the people of Largs. Facing the fountain is the former hotel that now forms a Benedictine Monastery. At one end of it is a Christian Heritage Museum and tearoom.

Further on is the Priory House Hotel followed by Curlinghall flats. These homes occupy the site of the Curlinghall Hotel, where Dr John Cairnie, founder of the Royal Caledonian Curling Club, established the first indoor curling rink in the world in January 1828.

Plaque on bridge

A second bay extends to the south of Cairnies Quay, overlooked by Broomfield Crescent. Warren Park Road is reached, but beyond this a pathway, known as the Bowen Craig Walk, follows the high water mark. It passes the Bowen Craigs, a series of rocks on the beach, and arrives at the Far Bowen Craigs, distinguished by its tall monument commemorating the Battle of Largs.

Ayrshire Coast-Battle of Largs

The Battle of Largs was the culmination of a series of raids on the west coast of Scotland by the Norse raiders. Alexander III, King of Scots, had tried to negotiate the return of the Hebrides to Scots control, but King Haco of Norway refused. Instead he made his way to Scotland where it was his intention to claim back lands that the Vikings had lost.

A fleet of 160 long ships, manned by anything from 2,000 to 20,000 Vikings, depending on which report is read, made its way up the Firth of Clyde. Alexander's men, who were much fewer in number, gathered on the Camp Hill west of Kilbirnie. A storm seems to have forced a few Viking boats onto the shore at Largs on 2 October 1263, whereupon they were attacked and repelled by the Scots. Haco sent more men to try and defend those in trouble, but they too were forced into a retreat. Haco later negotiated permission to bury the dead at the nearest Christian site, and this is thought to be at the Chapel of St Vey, on Little Cumbrae, where excavations in ancient cairns revealed numerous bones and steel helmets.

Though the battle was not of any major size, the victory was significant, and in its aftermath the Vikings loosened their claim to the Hebrides and accepted Alexander as their king. Two memorials commemorate the battle. "The Pencil" (illustrated on this page) was completed on 10 July 1912, a fine round tower on Far Bowen Craigs, designed by J.S. Kay. Much older is the standing stone in the garden at Curlinghall, which now bears a plaque.

Kelburn estate is one of the finest attractions on this part of the Ayrshire coast. The Boyles have owned the lands since 1140, and today it is the property of the Earl of Glasgow, chief of the clan. Kelburn Castle is a grand country seat, consisting of a tower house of 1581, to which a fine Queen Anne wing was added between 1692-1722. The house is open to the public during July and August.

The Kelburn estate boasts a fine country park, where there are numerous attractions to interest visitors. The former home farm is now the park

Kelburn Castle

centre, where there is a café and visitor centre. Within the grounds are adventure courses, a pet centre, and numerous walks, one of the most interesting being that which follows the Kel Burn itself, home to a number of fine waterfalls. Here also is a memorial to the 3rd Earl of Glasgow, by the illustrious Scottish architect Robert Adam (1728-92). The grounds also have the tallest Monterey Pine in Scotland and an amazing Weeping Larch, which covers half an acre.

David Boyle was an important Scots statesman, being created Lord Boyle in 1699 and Earl of Glasgow in 1703. He was a proponent of the Act of Union. The family fortunes were at one time considerable, but the 6th Earl found himself almost £1 million in debt.

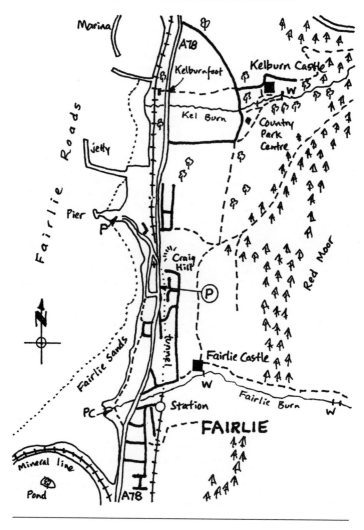

The village of Fairlie is attractively situated alongside a stretch of sands, overlooking Great Cumbrae. The railway arrived here in 1880, but the way further north was held up until the Fairlie Tunnel, at 4,000 yards one of the longest in southern Scotland, was excavated parallel to the main street. By 1885 the line was continued to Largs, with a siding to Fairlie Pier (1882), where a second station was opened, ready for pleasure steamers. This pier now has a play-park, car park, and sewage pumping station.

A second, more modern jetty, is located to the north of the old pier. This was constructed to allow NATO vessels to moor and take on supplies, but at the time of writing was derelict.

On the hill above the village stands the square tower of Fairlie Castle, erected in 1521. This was originally the seat of the Fairlies of that Ilk, who held it until the 18th century. The ballad "Hardyknute", by Elizabeth Halket, Lady Wardlaw (1677-1727), was set in this castle. The castle was until recently owned by the Boyles of Kelburn, but has been sold to a new owner who plans to restore it.

The old parish church in Fairlie dates from 1833. Within the vesti-
bule is an
ancient
carved
stone, de-
picting a
human
figure
and ani-
mals.

Fairlie Castle-view from south-east

Ayrshire Coast-Fairlie and Fife's yard

The west side of Bay Street is now occupied by modern housing, but originally was covered with a random selection of corrugated iron and brick sheds. This was home to the yard of William Fife and Son, which gained a world-wide reputation for boat building. The yard was established in 1812 and three generations of William Fifes designed and built over 800 fine yachts and other vessels until 1939.

The "Industry" was one of the earliest, constructed in 1814. The company specialised in racing yachts, and it was here that the Marquis of Ailsa's "Bloodhound" and "Shamrock" were built, as well as Sir Thomas Lipton's "Shamrock III". During the Second World War the yard was taken over by the Admiralty and used as the Anti-Submarine Experimental Establishment.

The yard continued for a number of years in other hands (known as Fairlie Yacht Slip Company) but finally closed in 1985, and was demolished to make way for housing.

A plaque commemorating the yard is affixed to the Village Inn and Mudhook Restaurant. This also commemorates the Mudhook Yacht Club that was founded here in 1873 by five Clyde yachtsmen.

"Altair" (1931)

At the southern end of Bay Street vehicles must return to the main road, but pedestrians can drop down the steps to the shore and make their way south along Fairlie Sands. The path continues for half a mile to the picnic area (conveniences) at the foot of Fairlie Burn, where the main road is rejoined. This route was originally the main road through the village.

At the southern end of Fairlie the coast is lost to the traveller due to the large terminal that has been constructed on the low-lying grounds of Fencefoot and Poteath. Part of Southannan Sands in Fence Bay has been incorporated in a vast area of ground that was used for the importation of iron ore, originally bound for the now-defunct Ravenscraig Steelworks at Motherwell. At one time there were plans to build a steelworks here, where large ore-carrying ships could unload directly into the factory, but they did not come to fruition. The terminal is now used for coal.

Southannan House was for a number of years a children's home, but today is falling into considerable disrepair. It occupies an ancient site, incorporating the remnants of Southannan Castle, extended in 1600 by Lord Semple "from a design which he procured in Italy, and was one of the most ambitious buildings built during the reign of James VI". Here also was a ruin known as St Annan's Chapel, which probably explains the name, there being no Northannan. On Diamond Hill above Southannan is a large rock with faint Bronze Age cup and ring markings. From Southannan the traveller must make his way along the A78 past Fencebay (smokehouse, restaurant and craft workshop) and Poteathbank Cottage to a large roundabout at the entrance to the Hunterston site. This spot is known as the Hunterston North Pillars.

From the south end of Fairlie one has to leave the coast behind to circumnavigate the Hunterston coal terminal. On passing beneath the high conveyor, turn right into the power station road.

Southannan House from the south

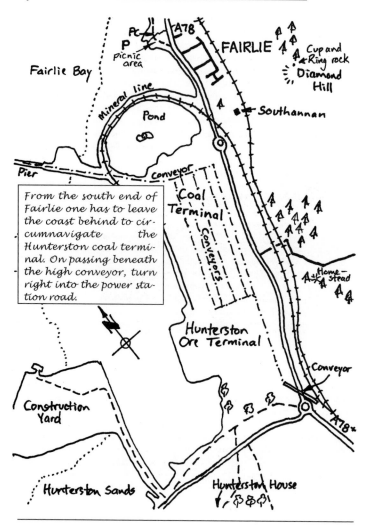

From the south end of Fairlie one has to leave the coast behind to circumnavigate the Hunterston coal terminal. On passing beneath the high conveyor, turn right into the power station road.

From Hunterston Gate North Pillars a wide roadway strikes west, signposted for Hunterston nuclear power station. On the right one soon sees the construction yard, built at the edge of Hunterston Sands, which adjoins the deep water in Fairlie Roads. To the left is Hunterston House, its view of Great Cumbrae partially restricted by industrial development.

The road passes the two nuclear power stations, Hunterston A and B. Cars can be taken as far as the pier below Hawking Craig, where a small area is designated for parking. The pier, which is 140 yards long, is used for landing material for the power stations, and no access is permitted. On the landward side is an enclosure used by BNFL for training purposes. A footpath continues along a raised beach below a mile-long cliff, known as Ardneil

The Three Sisters

Bank. The northern section is known as the Hawking Craig, and within the cliff is the historic Holy Cave, associated with St Kentigern or Mungo. This was used as a retreat from Glasgow, and the deep well was at one time a popular pilgrimage for its curative waters.

The Three Sisters is the name given to a cliff face that rises below Ardneil Hill. The cliffs are home to several challenging rock climbs. Opposite Northbank is Jenny's Dyke, a natural feature on the shore. The Pudding Rock is located in the woods of Ardneil Bank at a spot known as the Howgate.

A disused concrete pier is passed and one arrives in Portencross, a tiny but historic village.

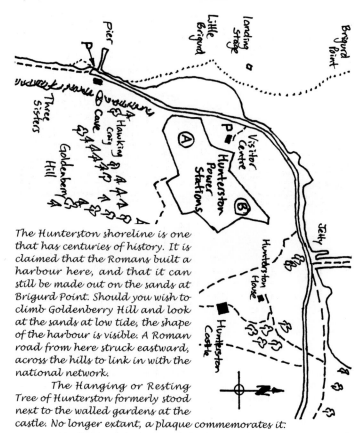

The Hunterston shoreline is one that has centuries of history. It is claimed that the Romans built a harbour here, and that it can still be made out on the sands at Brigurd Point. Should you wish to climb Goldenberry Hill and look at the sands at low tide, the shape of the harbour is visible. A Roman road from here struck eastward, across the hills to link in with the national network.

The Hanging or Resting Tree of Hunterston formerly stood next to the walled gardens at the castle. No longer extant, a plaque commemorates it:

"The Hunterston Resting Tree stood beside this wall for many years. A seat, where travellers could rest, was placed within the hollow trunk. In 1985 an oak seedling from Goldenberry wood was planted here by Neil Aylmer Hunter, 29th Laird of Hunterston and Chief of the Clan Hunter."

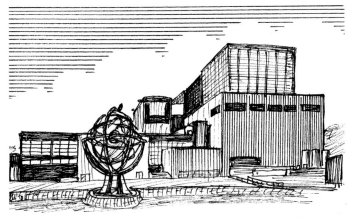

Hunterston B Station

There are two nuclear power stations at Hunterston, styled A and B. Hunterston A was a Magnox station which produced electricity from 1964 (when it was opened by HRH the Queen Mother) until 1990, when the second of two reactors was shut down. The building, which is distinguished by its massive glazed round towers, is now undergoing a process of decommissioning, which will take many years. There is a small visitor centre here.

Hunterston B is a less attractive building, little more than a huge box on the coastline. It was Scotland's first Advanced Gas-cooled Reactor station, and was commissioned in 1976. It can produce 1,170 megawatts of electricity, which is almost one quarter of the electrical requirements of Scotland.

Scottish Nuclear operates a visitor centre at Hunterston B that is open all year round, apart from Christmas and New Year. From here, guided tours of the power station are offered at regular intervals.

Other industry on this stretch of the coast includes a fish farm and an oil rig fabrication-yard. The latter is located on a man-made island in the deep waters of Fairlie Roads, reached by a half-mile long causeway.

Ayrshire Coast-Hunterston Castle and House

The oldest part of Hunterston Castle dates from the 15th century, but the original square tower was extended in the 17th century. The castle was abandoned as the family seat of the Hunter family when Hunterston House was erected around 1799, but in 1913 the tower was restored to the plans of Sir Robert Lorimer. Today the castle remains the property of Hunter of Hunterston, chief of the clan.

Hunterston Castle

A parchment signed by King Robert II on 2 May 1374 confirms the grant of these lands to the Hunter family. The chief must pay the monarch a silver penny on the Feast of Pentecost should he arrive at Hunterston and so the present chief keeps a few old pennies of Robert II and George V, just in case.

The Hunters get their name from being the hereditary keepers of the royal hunting forests on Arran and Little Cumbrae. The family played its part in the history of Scotland: John, the 14th laird, died at Flodden; Mungo, the 16th laird, died at Pinkie; Sir Aylmer Hunter-Weston was a distinguished soldier and MP.

In the grounds is the ancient Hunter yew tree, used for making bows. It is reputed to be the second oldest in Scotland, perhaps planted in 1110 when the Hunters first acquired the lands.

One of the strangest murder cases took place on this lonely stretch of coast in 1913. In May of that year three people moved into Northbank Cottage, which lies a few hundred yards north of Portencross. They were Alexander MacLaren and his wife, Jessie, and his sister-in-law, Miss Mary Speir Gunn. The three were sitting in the cottage on the evening of Saturday 18 October. Alexander MacLaren was reading aloud from a book by WW Jacobs when suddenly the peace was shattered. A shot was fired, smashing the window, and the bullet hit Miss Gunn. She cried out, "Oh Alex, I'm shot," before falling to the ground. More shots rang out, one wounding Mrs MacLaren. When the shooting stopped, Alexander left the cottage and searched outside. No one was visible, and the dogs in the kennels had not barked as they usually did when a stranger was about. MacLaren ran to Portencross to raise the alarm.

The police and doctor arrived at the cottage where they found Mrs MacLaren shot in the back, and Miss Gunn dead, having been hit by three bullets. Three sets of footprints and a further bullet were discovered outside the broken window.

Intensive enquiries by the police came to nothing. They investigated as far away as Saskatchewan in Canada, where Miss Gunn had a boyfriend for a time, but no suspects or motives were ever discovered. Even a reward of £100 brought forth no information and the murder remains unsolved to this day.

Northbank Cottage

In 1826 two workmen were digging ditches at the base of the Hawking Craig when they found a rather fine looking brooch. At first they were unsure what it was, but on cleaning its significance became clear.

What they had discovered was probably one of the most magnificent artefacts ever to be unearthed in Scotland. It was made of solid silver and ornamented with gold filigree and inset with amber. It was dated to around AD 700. A 10th century runic inscription on the back was translated as "Malbritha owns this brooch". It is thought the brooch was the work of Anglo-Saxon craftsmen, based somewhere in the west of Scotland or else in Ireland, where the Celtic designs proved to be a considerable influence.

The brooch, now fully restored to its original condition, is on display in the National Museum of Scotland in Edinburgh, though a replica is held at Hunterston. The museum originally paid £500 for the brooch in 1891.

Hunterston Brooch

The north harbour looking towards the concrete pier

Portencross is a tiny village located at the west end of the B7048. However, the village has a distinguished history, and tradition holds that it was here the bodies of the Scots royal family left the mainland en route to burial at Iona. The castle is the main feature of the village, but in the woods below Auld Hill stands Auchenames House, at one time a seat of the Crauford family, but sold around 1900 to the Adams. The house was probably built around 1800, when it was known as the North Cottage, but following extensions in 1839 (including the garden and belfry) it was given its present name.

Auld Hill itself is topped by a prehistoric fort and dun, the dun being described in early accounts as a circular watch tower.

Portencross has two small, yet charming, harbours. The Old Harbour lies next to the castle, whereas the North Harbour lies a hundred yards to the north, below Auchenames. Both are, in essence, little more than inlets of the sea, delineated by drystone walls.

In 1588 one of the Spanish Armada's vessels sank off Portencross in ten fathoms of water. It is said that a local witch was responsible for the sinking. A cannon from this ship long stood on the Castle Green.

In the 1960s there were proposals to erect an oil refinery here. Standard Oil (Esso) proposed a facility that could cope with 10 million tons of oil, but fortunately this did not materialise.

Ayrshire Coast-Portencross Castle

Portencross Castle is one of Ayrshire's finest ruins, standing on a low rock headland that juts into the sea. The castle is L-shaped in plan, but the jamb is found on the short side of the main block, rather than on the long side, which is more common. The ground floor is vaulted, the two kitchens being located in the wing. A spiral stair leads up to the first floor, which contains a great vaulted hall, 24 feet by 16, rising over 19 feet to the top of the vault. Large windows with bench seating overlook the tiny landing place on the beach.

Portencross Castle was the main seat (or caput) of the Barony of Ardneil. The lands were granted by Robert the Bruce in 1306 to Sir Robert Boyd of Kilmarnock. The king actually visited the castle on many occasions, signing a number of charters there. It remained in Boyd hands until 1737. However, by this time it was occupied by "fishermen and other inferior tenants" until January 1739 when it was unroofed in a storm.

The castle became the property of the electricity companies at Hunterston, but in 1998 it was put up for sale and is likely to be the subject of a restoration project, with a view to it being re-occupied.

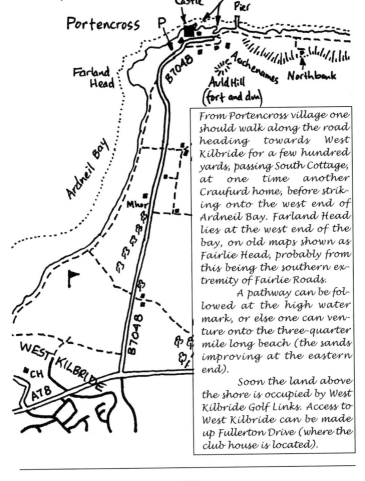

From Portencross village one should walk along the road heading towards West Kilbride for a few hundred yards, passing South Cottage, at one time another Craufurd home, before striking onto the west end of Ardneil Bay. Farland Head lies at the west end of the bay, on old maps shown as Fairlie Head, probably from this being the southern extremity of Fairlie Roads.

A pathway can be followed at the high water mark, or else one can venture onto the three-quarter mile long beach (the sands improving at the eastern end).

Soon the land above the shore is occupied by West Kilbride Golf Links. Access to West Kilbride can be made up Fullerton Drive (where the club house is located).

Ayrshire Coast-Seamill

At the foot of Fullerton Drive stands the red sandstone Redholme House. Beyond here one has to venture onto the shore to walk further, but it is a pleasant sandy stroll. Access to Seamill is possible via Sandy Road, which allows vehicles onto the beach. Seamill Hydro Hotel (1871 but extended) stands on the shore here, a tall wall protecting it from the waves. It is possible to walk past the hotel, and round a narrow pathway at the foot of the Kilbride Burn to a footbridge at the Sea Mill itself. Again, access to the main road can be made past Tarbet House, though most folk will prefer to walk along the path behind the Ardrossan Road houses towards Chapelton Mains

The Sea Mill lies at the foot of the Kilbride Burn, just short of its confluence with the sea. The present double-storey rubble building may date from around 1790 and retains its smallish iron and wood millwheel. The pond originally stored water for the mill.

Sea Mill

On the opposite side of the road from the Sea Mill are the vestiges of a prehistoric fort, known as the Castle Hill, now largely altered due to the erection of a house named The Fort. During a partial excavation charcoal, cattle bones and antlers were unearthed. In 1833 two prehistoric urns were discovered when the road was being realigned near here

Seamill became popular with holidaymakers, and those who could afford to build themselves holiday homes. In 1893 a large convalescent home was opened by the Glasgow and West of Scotland co-operative societies in Glenbride Road. This is now a Christian outdoor centre.

The path behind the Seamill bungalows returns to the A78 at the sewage pumping station.

Chapelton Mains (now houses) occupies the gap between the forking roads at the south end of Seamill. On the lands of this farm in 1871, 300 silver coins from the reign of Queen Elizabeth I were found.

It is possible to avoid the main road for a bit and keep to the coast between Seamill and the Waterside Inn by following the coast outwith the fence. This wends round the two low headlands known as the North and South Inches.

The road makes its way across the raised beach to Ardrossan, just over three miles from Seamill. In the woods above Glenfoot House Hotel is a prehistoric homestead; a dun occupies a similar position below Boydston, and a Norman motte hill rises above the Montfode Burn.

This part of the coast is known as Boydston Shore. On the sands, at low water, ancient fish traps can be discerned, created by erecting stone dikes to catch the fish as the tide recedes.

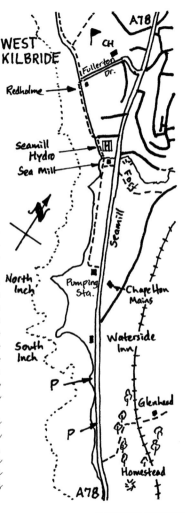

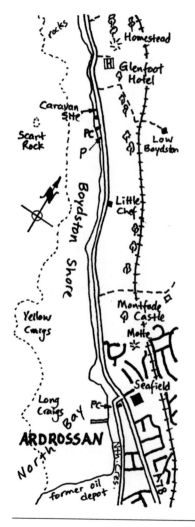

Five hundred yards up Montfode farm road can be seen the remains of Montfode Castle, little more than a round tower containing a few shot holes. The castle was the seat of the Montfode of that Ilk family.

The north-west end of Ardrossan (Eglinton Road and North Crescent Road) is home to a few salubrious private houses. On entering the town one soon reaches the open grasslands of Eglinton Road (toilets), overlooking the beach and Long Craigs. Seafield School is a Quarriers' establishment. A baronial-cum-Jacobean building, Seafield was originally built in 1820 for Mrs Bartlemore but extended to its present guise for W.G. Barron in 1858 and for A.D. Bryce-Douglas in 1880.

Just before Seafield's gates are reached, the pedestrian should strike to the right, into North Crescent Road, which can be followed past the site of the oil depot (now Harbour Industrial Estate) to Montgomerie Street. This runs parallel with the main thoroughfare in the old part of the town, Glasgow Street.

Out in Ardrossan's North Bay is the intriguing Horse Isle. The island is not particularly large, spreading over 12 acres at high tide, but it performs a useful task in protecting the harbour from some of the worst westerlies.

The island's name is said to derive "from ye surname of Horsse of ye Philipe Horsse, sone-in-law to Sir Richard Morwell, who, in old evidents, wes stylled Phillipus de Horssey, Janitor Comitis Gallovidiae." Others, however, claim that the island was used as a place of quarantine for horses being imported.

Horse Isle beacon

Rising from the rocks on Horse Isle is a 52 feet tall beacon, visible from the mainland. This was erected in 1811 by Hugh, Earl of Eglinton, at the suggestion of Sir John Ross, the celebrated Arctic explorer. In the early 1800s the sailors from north Ayrshire ports had petitioned the Commissioners of Lighthouses to erect a proper lighthouse, but this was never built.

At the north west point of the island is the Sheep Port. Tradition has it that cattle and sheep were landed here from the western islands before being brought ashore and driven to market on the mainland.

Horse Isle and its two lesser islets - North and East - are today protected as a nature reserve by the Royal Society for the Protection of Birds. Here seals and seabirds find a pleasant refuge. However, the island's breeding tern population has dwindled from hundreds down to a few pairs. The RSPB carries out an annual census of breeding birds, and in 1998 found almost 3,000 nests, belonging to gulls, eider, swans, geese, and other varieties.

Ayrshire Coast-Ardrossan Harbour

The 12th Earl of Eglinton created the harbour at Ardrossan and the foundation stone was laid on 31 May 1806. His successor, the 13th Earl, continued the work of development. The proposals for a canal from here to Glasgow did not come to fruition, despite plans by Thomas Telford in 1805.

The first cargo to arrive came aboard the brig "Helen" that brought timber from Salem Bay in North America. In 1863 the harbour was officially designated a port.

The Ardrossan Harbour Company later took over and, between 1886 and 1891, constructed the Eglinton Dock and Basin and a new breakwater.

The harbour was so important that it once had two railway stations operated by different companies - one on Montgomerie Pier, the other on Winton Pier. Only the latter remains (now known as Ardrossan Harbour station).

A dock that could be closed by locks formerly existed where the Arran ferry now berths, into which were slips from the Ardrossan shipyard. The building with the tower in the illustration above is the Power House of 1892.

The harbour today is more of a tourist resort, for here the car ferry for Brodick on the Island of Arran leaves every two hours. The Eglinton Dock has been converted into a yachting marina, with berthing for all craft up to 100 feet in length.

The ancient castle of Ardrossan stands on the Castle Hill, a significant mound located in the centre of the town. The ruins are of a considerable size, but the stronghold must have been much larger at one time.

Some historians believe that Sir William Wallace, the great Scots freedom fighter, set a house near to the castle on fire. When the English soldiers, who held the castle at that time, came out to extinguish the flames they discovered it was a trick and were swiftly put to the sword. Indeed, so many Englishmen were killed that Wallace packed the bodies into a vault in the castle, still known as Wallace's Larder.

In the 17th century Oliver Cromwell used stones from the tower to build the Citadel at Ayr. The stones were probably taken down the hillside and loaded onto boats that then sailed to the county town.

Also to be found on Castle Hill are the remnants of the old church of Ardrossan and its graveyard. A stone coffin lid, which is finely decorated with a floral cross, was found here and is now located in the town hall. Also on the hill top, overlooking the town, is an obelisk memorial commemorating Dr Alexander MacFadzean (1788-1849), who was instrumental in having Ardrossan designated as a burgh.

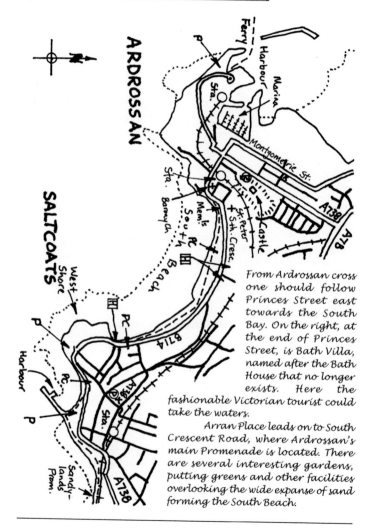

From Ardrossan cross one should follow Princes Street east towards the South Bay. On the right, at the end of Princes Street, is Bath Villa, named after the Bath House that no longer exists. Here the fashionable Victorian tourist could take the waters.

Arran Place leads on to South Crescent Road, where Ardrossan's main Promenade is located. There are several interesting gardens, putting greens and other facilities overlooking the wide expanse of sand forming the South Beach.

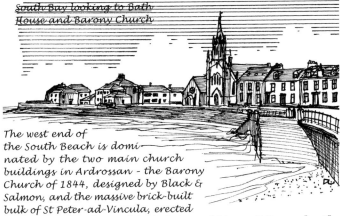

South Bay looking to Bath House and Barony Church

The west end of the South Beach is dominated by the two main church buildings in Ardrossan - the Barony Church of 1844, designed by Black & Salmon, and the massive brick-built bulk of St Peter-ad-Vincula, erected in 1938 to the plans of Jack Coia and Warnett Kennedy. The Barony Church is a plain gothic block with the addition of a rather grand, but squat, spire, containing a clock. St Peter's has a brick tower, and the whole building is a study in red - red brick, slates and paint on the doors and windows!

Across the road is the War Memorial, which is in the form of a large Celtic cross. Adorned with carvings, it commemorates the dead of two world wars.

Near to the war memorial, in a sunken garden area, is a huge boulder with a plaque that reads:

> *This memorial is dedicated to the officers and men who Perished when HMS "Dasher", an Archer class aircraft carrier, Sank on 27th March 1943. "We will remember them".*

The "Dasher" was built in the United States in 1940 but was acquired by the Royal Navy. After completing exercises off Arran, the vessel was heading for Glasgow when an explosion occurred on board. The ship sank within six minutes, with the loss of 379 officers and crew.

Facing the bay are some rather fine double storey buildings, some of which are now hotels, as well as modern flats.

Where the B714 (Burn Road) strikes off the A738 (Ardrossan Road) one passes almost without noticing from Ardrossan into Saltcoats (the Stanley Burn actually forms the boundary at this point). Burn Road soon becomes Montgomerie Crescent, a fine sweep of houses overlooking Saltcoats West Shore, with views back to Ardrossan. Walkers will prefer to follow the Promenade at the sea wall.

Montgomerie Crescent itself then becomes Winton Circus at a small park area, overlooked by Melbourne Terrace. Here can be found public conveniences

Winton Circus reaches out towards the headland on which Saltcoats was built. The headland used to have three ponds on it, a Model Yachting Pond, Bathing Pool and one other, but the fun of sea-bathing has long-since passed, and a new leisure pool is located east of the town at Auchenharvie.

The road continues round the corner (now Braes Road) with views across Saltcoats harbour. The landward side of the harbour is occupied by a large car park for Saltcoats town centre, which is a popular shopping area, complete with market. The main street is now pedestrianised.

The North Ayrshire Museum is located in the former mid 18th century parish church, still standing in its kirkyard. Numerous mementoes of the past are on display, including local and national exhibits, as well as temporary exhibitions.

Anchor on Saltcoats harbour-side

The harbour at Saltcoats is of no great size, but was at one time a port of some significance. The natural headland forms the west side of the harbour, the east protected by a projecting pier known as The Shott (originally erected in the 17th century), beyond which is the little New Pier (of 1914). The harbour is protected to the east by the tall wall, through which a narrow doorway leads down to the rocks. Access to the harbour for boats is made through two rocks known as the Inner and Outer Nebbocks. The harbour was used mainly for the export of coal from the mines in the vicinity.

In the bay of the harbour can sometimes be seen fossilized tree stumps. These were first discovered when the sands were washed away for a time following a storm. The stumps are similar, but smaller to those that can be seen in Glasgow's Fossil Grove.

Along the harbour promenade (parking) can be seen a large anchor, a sundial depicting Saltcoats Local Time and a bandstand. At the west end, where once were open-air swimming baths, can be found amusements and a funfair. The town centre is just a short walk away.

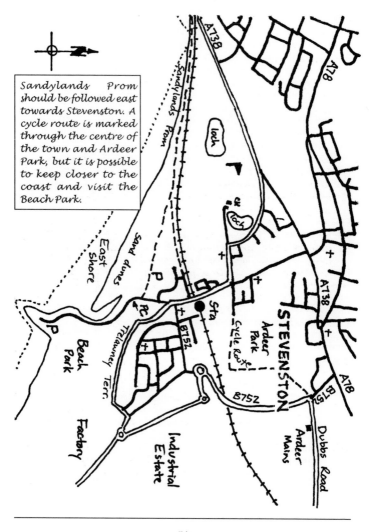

Sandylands Prom should be followed east towards Stevenston. A cycle route is marked through the centre of the town and Ardeer Park, but it is possible to keep closer to the coast and visit the Beach Park.

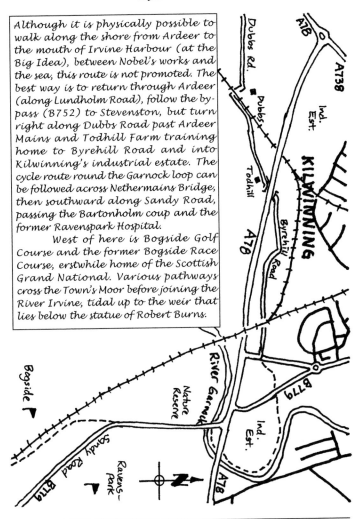

Although it is physically possible to walk along the shore from Ardeer to the mouth of Irvine Harbour (at the Big Idea), between Nobel's works and the sea, this route is not promoted. The best way is to return through Ardeer (along Lundholm Road), follow the by-pass (B752) to Stevenston, but turn right along Dubbs Road past Ardeer Mains and Todhill Farm training home to Byrehill Road and into Kilwinning's industrial estate. The cycle route round the Garnock loop can be followed across Nethermains Bridge, then southward along Sandy Road, passing the Bartonholm coup and the former Ravenspark Hospital.

West of here is Bogside Golf Course and the former Bogside Race Course, erstwhile home of the Scottish Grand National. Various pathways cross the Town's Moor before joining the River Irvine, tidal up to the weir that lies below the statue of Robert Burns.

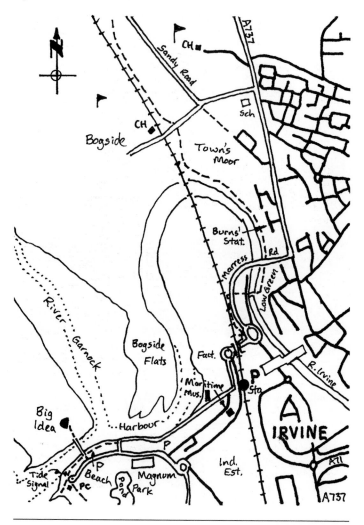

The cycle route should be followed through the busy centre of Irvine. From Irvine Golf Club (Bogside) it follows the railway for a short stretch before striking along the top of the River Irvine, alongside the Town's Moor. Soon the statue of Robert Burns is reached.

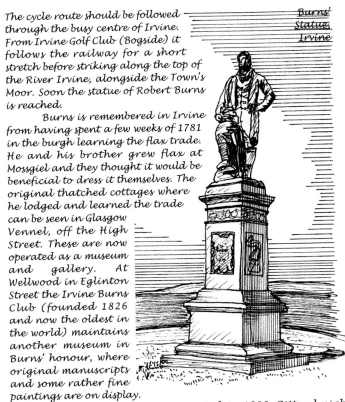

Burns' Statue, Irvine

Burns is remembered in Irvine from having spent a few weeks of 1781 in the burgh learning the flax trade. He and his brother grew flax at Mossgiel and they thought it would be beneficial to dress it themselves. The original thatched cottages where he lodged and learned the trade can be seen in Glasgow Vennel, off the High Street. These are now operated as a museum and gallery. At Wellwood in Eglinton Street the Irvine Burns Club (founded 1826 and now the oldest in the world) maintains another museum in Burns' honour, where original manuscripts and some rather fine paintings are on display.

The statue of Burns was erected in 1896. Pittendreigh MacGillivray sculpted it.

A few cobblestones in the grass between the statue and Marress Road mark the site of the former burgh gallows, where two Covenanters were hanged in 1666 for their religious beliefs. They are buried in the town's old kirkyard.

The cycle path should be followed below the Marress Bridge onto Irvine's Low Green.

The cycle path enters the north end of the Low Green. This was at one time Irvine's common, where lime was quarried and coal was mined before it became a public open space.

The path crosses the footbridge, arriving at an isolated row of houses known as Waterside. These are often subject to flooding. The path continues under Marress Road before turning south, wending its way between the main road and the railway line. It then arrives at Fullarton Parish Church. This is a rather unusual Gothic style building, dating from 1837 and designed by James Ingram. The church hall was a former school building of 1840.

On the other side of the street is the glass-roofed Marress House, used for tax offices, and Cunningham House, location of council offices and the library. Beyond this is the large Rivergate shopping centre, which straddles the River Irvine.

The route passes beneath the railway bridge and round the outside edge of Victoria Roundabout into Cochrane Street. A sharp right brings one into Montgomery Street. This is quite an attractive street, and one that has been restored to its former glory, with decent modern buildings infilling the gaps, notably the "Bookends" at the north eastern end.

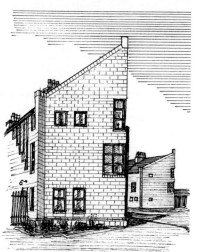

The Bookends, Montgomery Street

The street was named after James Montgomery (1771-1854), who wrote many hymns and religious poems. He was born at 26 Montgomery Street, the son of a Moravian minister. He became a journalist and editor in Sheffield, but spent three months in York Castle prison for printing a seditious poem and later another six months for reporting a riot.

Irvine harbour was at one time one of the busiest on the west coast of Scotland. Here ships landed timber, oats, butter, fruit and hides, and exported coal, tanned leather, chrome ore and fireclay products. At the head of the harbour was a notable shipyard.

Today the harbour is home to pleasure craft and a range of attractions designed with the visitor in mind. The Scottish Maritime Museum is based here, and it has an extensive display of artefacts and vessels. Tickets for the museum allow visitors to examine the boats still afloat, to look around the Linthouse engine

The "Spartan"

shop (transported from Govan in Glasgow), the shipyard worker's tenement house in Montgomery Street, and the other facilities. The vessels preserved here include the puffer "Spartan", fishing boat "Antares" (which was lifted from the seabed), sailing ship "Carrick" and the Longhope lifeboat.

The houses along the harbour side are a mix of old and new, and in most cases the new has been designed to blend in with the surroundings. Nearby is the well-equipped and very popular Magnum leisure centre which offers a wide range of indoor sports and games. Old inns and pubs can be found along the harbourside, most offering meals.

A few sculptures can be seen, including the statue of the carter and his horse, and an amusing stone carving depicting a fisherman trying to pull his net of fish through a massive wave!

Ship Inn

The Ship Inn is located on the harbour front and is a popular place for refreshments and meals. The inn is actually the oldest in the town, being built in 1597, using whinstone transported from near Dundonald. At that time the inn was an ostlers and stables, but was rebuilt in 1754 and in that year received its first licence. Typically Scots in style, the Ship Inn is distinguished by its large cut-away corner, which was designed to allow for easier traffic flow.

The owner at the time the licence was issued was Charles Hamilton, born in 1704 and a son of the laird of Ladyland in Kilbirnie parish. He was employed as a tidewaiter for the excise in 1740 and became Collector of Customs for Irvine port, with a staff of fourteen. He was also enrolled as a burgess as well as a town councillor. Hamilton had for many years a monopoly over the sale of alcohol at Irvine harbour. He lived in the town, but his job earned him enough to facilitate the purchase of Garvoch estate in Renfrewshire, and he inherited Craighlaw Castle in Wigtownshire from his elder brother. Hamilton was friendly with Robert Burns when the poet stayed in the town, and he was provost of the town between 1758 and 1781. He died in 1783.

There are other inns and pubs along the harbour front, the Keys being the furthest out. The harbour master's office is the last structure in the street, only the tide signal building standing beyond it. At one time the lifeboat station stood where a breakwater sticks out to sea.

The Big Idea

At the south-eastern tip of the Ardeer peninsula, but accessible from Irvine harbour-side by a retractable bridge, is the fascinating visitor attraction known as The Big Idea, the world's first inventor centre. It was constructed in the late 1990s in a distinctive style, and consists of a large dome partly covered by grass, the open slice distinguished by its glazing. From the sea the dome merges into the Ardeer dunes, but beneath can be found one of the most exciting visitor experiences in the district. The centre opened in 1999, and is operated by the Nobel Exhibition Trust. It is open to the public all year round, apart from Christmas and New Year.

The Big Idea was developed to celebrate the success of Scottish inventions, and visitors are invited to have a go at inventing and discovering things for themselves. The "Bridge of Scottish Invention" has details of 23 Scottish inventors on it, and while the casual visitor may not know some of the names, it is well worth investigating to discover what they were responsible for. Should a boat need to navigate up or down river then the Ardeer side of the bridge rolls back to allow it to pass.

Within the dome are areas dedicated to all sorts of inventions, from the earliest of times to the space age. Visitors are given a special key that allows them to interact with the exhibits. The Big Idea also has a gift shop and café.

Ayrshire Coast-Automatic Tide Signal

The unique tower at the mouth of the harbour was erected in 1906 as an automatic tide signal. The tower has four storeys and is topped by a flat roof. Sticking out of the top of this is a tall cross-shaped mast that originally had a number of spherical balls hanging from it. By looking at the balls one could tell how the tide was at the foot of the River Irvine which was, and still is, a notorious spot to navigate, the depth of water dropping to as little as a couple of feet at low tides.

This system of gauging the depth of water was invented by the harbourmaster, Martin Boyd. In tanks by the quayside were floats connected by chains and pulleys to the foot of the tower.

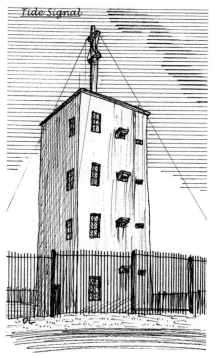

Tide Signal

Within were ropes that pulled the balls up through the roof, the principle being that a greater water depth was indicated by a higher number of visible balls.

To allow the harbour to function at night, lamps were located behind the small windows on the seaward side, and the same system of pulleys pulled up screens, which covered the windows with either red or black covers. The light pattern again indicated the depth of water at the Bar.

Today the tower is disused, but a very small gauge railway system (or large model railway) uses the enclosure and part of the surrounding grassland.

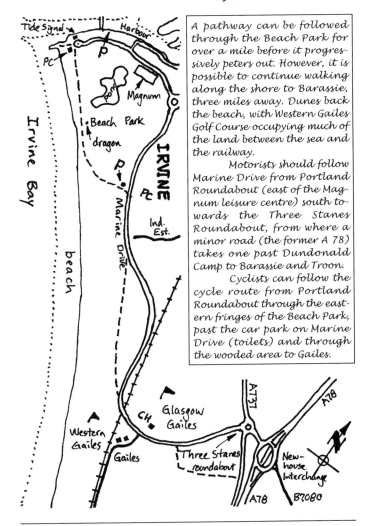

A pathway can be followed through the Beach Park for over a mile before it progressively peters out. However, it is possible to continue walking along the shore to Barassie, three miles away. Dunes back the beach, with Western Gailes Golf Course occupying much of the land between the sea and the railway.

Motorists should follow Marine Drive from Portland Roundabout (east of the Magnum leisure centre) south towards the Three Stanes Roundabout, from where a minor road (the former A78) takes one past Dundonald Camp to Barassie and Troon.

Cyclists can follow the cycle route from Portland Roundabout through the eastern fringes of the Beach Park, past the car park on Marine Drive (toilets) and through the wooded area to Gailes.

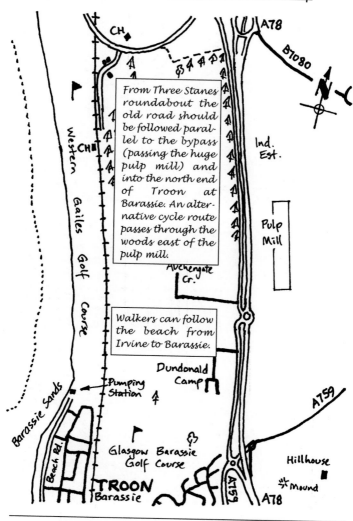

From Three Stanes roundabout the old road should be followed parallel to the bypass (passing the huge pulp mill) and into the north end of Troon at Barassie. An alternative cycle route passes through the woods east of the pulp mill.

Walkers can follow the beach from Irvine to Barassie.

A78

B1080

N

Western Gailes Golf Course

CH

CH

Ind. Est.

Pulp Mill

Auchengate Cr.

Dundonald Camp

A759

Pumping Station

Barassie Sands

Beach Rd.

Glasgow Barassie Golf Course

TROON
Barassie

Hillhouse

Mound

A759

A78

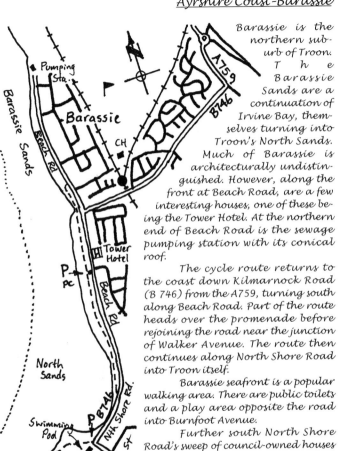

Barassie is the northern suburb of Troon. The Barassie Sands are a continuation of Irvine Bay, themselves turning into Troon's North Sands. Much of Barassie is architecturally undistinguished. However, along the front at Beach Road, are a few interesting houses, one of these being the Tower Hotel. At the northern end of Beach Road is the sewage pumping station with its conical roof.

The cycle route returns to the coast down Kilmarnock Road (B 746) from the A759, turning south along Beach Road. Part of the route heads over the promenade before rejoining the road near the junction of Walker Avenue. The route then continues along North Shore Road into Troon itself.

Barassie seafront is a popular walking area. There are public toilets and a play area opposite the road into Burnfoot Avenue.

Further south North Shore Road's sweep of council-owned houses is visible, in a rather distinguished location, and forming an elegant arch around the bay. Beyond this point, one arrives in the attractive and affluent town of Troon.

At Troon Leisure Pool on North Shore Road, walkers and cyclists can make their way through the park and rejoin the road at Templehill. Motorists need to head to the town centre and turn right, down the main shopping area in Portland Street. At the traffic lights one should turn right, into Templehill, where shops, the Anchorage Hotel and toilets are located.

Those who wish to keep as close to the coast as possible will find that the promontory at Troon gives them an extra two miles. Some of this is unattractive, as it passes the wood yards and massive sheds of Ailsa Troon shipbuilding yard, but here the visitor can experience the bustle of a working harbour. Troon Marina, a mass of yachts tied up alongside jetties, now occupies most of the inner basin. The Troon Cruising Club has its base here.

Beyond the shipyard is the busy fish market, moved here from Ayr. It stands alongside a smaller basin, home to a number of inshore fishing boats and a hive of activity at most times. Troon lifeboat station is also located here. Further on, at the very tip of the nose after which Troon gets its name ("An t-Sron" in Gaelic) is the terminal for ferries to Northern Ireland.

A small row of cottages that now form offices stand by the side of a small road that leads to the outer shore of the point. Cars need to be left at the parking areas at the foot of this road, but cyclists and walkers can enjoy one of Troon's most delightful spots. An old anchor from some ship or other is lying on a stone circle by the roadside.

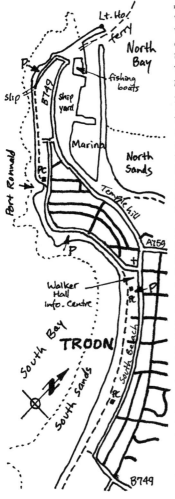

At the car park at the anchor, where there is a slip down to the waterside, a pathway begins to climb up a grass mound. This is the northern end of the Ballast Bank, a massive mound created from ballast that came from ships returning to port. The bank was started in 1840 by the Duke of Portland to protect the new harbour that he had established here in 1808. Before the bank had been created the harbour was too exposed to gales from the west, resulting in a few ships being wrecked whilst using it.

The pathway along the bank gives views over the harbour area and across the town to the Dundonald hills. To the west there is a splendid view over the firth to Arran, the little Lady Isle looking something like a submarine in certain conditions. Although there is a light beacon, it has caused a few shipwrecks over the years. The isle is now protected as a nature reserve for birds, and is home to a colony of grey seals.

The path on the bank drops back to shore level at Port Ronnald, a small shingly bay at the foot of Kennedy Road (toilets). One then walks along Titchfield Road into Troon's South Bay and the South Beach Esplanade.

South Beach Hotel

At the northern end of South Beach is the site of Troon's former open-air swimming pool, now filled in and used as a car park. Beyond is an area of grassland between the double-storey houses and the shore, forming the South Beach Esplanade. At St Clair Terrace is a granite memorial fountain presented to the town in 1891 by James Dickie. Walkers and cyclists can make their way along the promenade to the southern end of the town.

One of the most distinguished buildings passed here is the Troon Council Chambers, a massive Georgian-styled building dating from 1932 and the work of James Miller. Here also is a seasonal tourist-information-centre. The Walker Hall (1954) was the gift of whisky baron Sir Alexander Walker to Troon. Walker, son of the famous "Johnnie Walker", lived at Piersland House, which is now another hotel, located in Craigend Road.

Next to the halls is the burgh War Memorial, a sizeable bronze statue of Britannia overlooking the bay. This was the work of Alfred Gilbert. Near to it are public toilets.

The South Beach Esplanade can be followed along the shore to its terminus at Craigend Road. The houses in South Beach itself (B749) are distinguished Georgian buildings, but which turn their back on the dunes and shore, sheltering from the winter storms. Some of these have been converted into hotels. Along the shore is a stone with the inscribed: "Northern Boundary of the Port of Ayr". A parking area is located at the southern end of the esplanade.

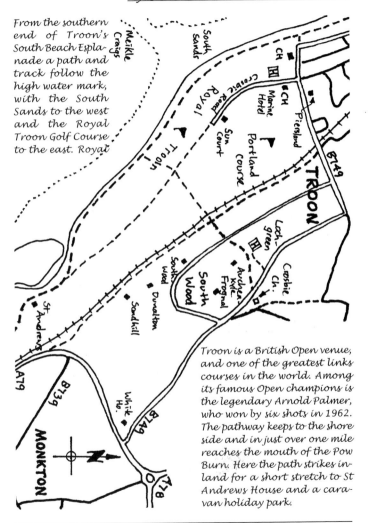

From the southern end of Troon's South Beach Esplanade a path and track follow the high water mark, with the South Sands to the west and the Royal Troon Golf Course to the east. Royal

Meikle Craigs

South Sands

Crosbie Road

CH

H

Marine Hotel

CH

Piersland

Royal Troon

Sun Court

Portland Course

B749

TROON

Loch-green

H

South Wood

Archer-kvile Frognal

Crosbie Ch.

South Wood

Dundonton

Sandkill

St Andrews

A79

B739

White Ho.

B749

B78

MONKTON

Troon is a British Open venue, and one of the greatest links courses in the world. Among its famous Open champions is the legendary Arnold Palmer, who won by six shots in 1962. The pathway keeps to the shore side and in just over one mile reaches the mouth of the Pow Burn. Here the path strikes inland for a short stretch to St Andrews House and a caravan holiday park.

Ayrshire Coast-Troon to St Andrew's House

There are a few alternative routes here. One can be found a few hundred yards inland, at first following Crosbie Road. It passes the Marine Hotel, a large Victorian pile and one of the finest hotels in Scotland. On the opposite side of the road is the clubhouse for Troon Portland Golf Course. The road continues for almost half a mile to the former Sun Court Hotel, the east side of the road being the location of a number of distinguished dwelling houses. The Sun Court building was renowned for having one of only two Real tennis courts in Scotland, but is now a nursing home.

From here a track through the centre of the golf course can be followed to a small building about half a mile from the end of the public road, after which there is only a pathway to St Andrew's House, which is easily seen 800 yards away.

Cyclists require to follow the cycle route that heads inland and follows Craigend Road before turning right on the east side of the railway bridge. The route then runs alongside the railway for a mile and a half before reaching the bypass at Prestwick Airport. This route was opened in 2001 and passes alongside the South Wood, the most prestigious address in Ayrshire and location of a number of magnificent houses. A number of these were built in the neo-baronial style, including Lochgreen (1905), Auchenkyle (c.1905), Dunalton (1908), Frognal (1909) and Southwood (1905). Sandhill House is older, originally built for the Dowager Duchess of Portland around 1890.

Lochgreen House

A road bridge over the railway can be crossed and cars taken as far as the bridge over the Rumbling Burn, at the gates to Prestwick Holiday Park. This caravan site (mostly static vans) was originally an army camp, established during the Second World War. For a number of years a Polish unit was in occupation. They were later to erect a war memorial on this site, which latterly suffered from vandalism but was later restored and moved to Stonegarth House, now the RAFA club, on Prestwick Esplanade.

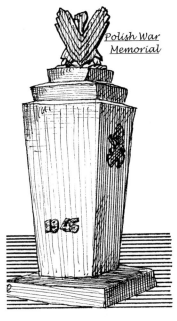

Polish War Memorial

St Andrew's House was originally known as Monkton House, although this name was also used for Orangefield House, which was later adapted as the original terminal and traffic control centre for Prestwick Airport.

It was in the immediate area that a team of smugglers operated in the 18th century. The beach at the foot of the Pow Burn was a suitably secluded spot for their nefarious activities. Here brandy and rum were run ashore and concealed at places known as Rum How or Brandy Hill. In the early 19th century whisky illegally distilled on the island of Arran was landed on this spot. In Ayrshire, the spirit was euphemistically known as "Arran Water".

In the 18th century the shore from Prestwick to Troon was an alternative roadway (probably to avoid the tolls), but "there is a dangerous quick sand on the road at the foot of the Pow Burn to avoid it keep as near the sea as the tide will allow", according to Armstrong's map of the county.

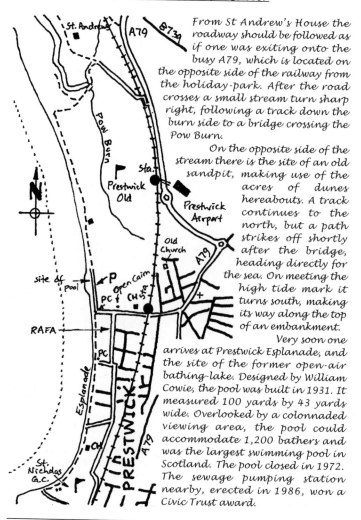

From St Andrew's House the roadway should be followed as if one was exiting onto the busy A79, which is located on the opposite side of the railway from the holiday-park. After the road crosses a small stream turn sharp right, following a track down the burn side to a bridge crossing the Pow Burn.

On the opposite side of the stream there is the site of an old sandpit, making use of the acres of dunes hereabouts. A track continues to the north, but a path strikes off shortly after the bridge, heading directly for the sea. On meeting the high tide mark it turns south, making its way along the top of an embankment.

Very soon one arrives at Prestwick Esplanade, and the site of the former open-air bathing-lake. Designed by William Cowie, the pool was built in 1931. It measured 100 yards by 43 yards wide. Overlooked by a colonnaded viewing area, the pool could accommodate 1,200 bathers and was the largest swimming pool in Scotland. The pool closed in 1972. The sewage pumping station nearby, erected in 1986, won a Civic Trust award.

Straddling the Pow Burn is Prestwick Golf Club's famous course. It originally had only 12 holes, when "Old" Tom Morris laid it out in the 1850s. Here, on 17 October 1860, the very first Open Championship competition was held. The club put up a belt as the trophy, but invited only Scottish professionals to compete. As a

17th hole, Old Prestwick

result, the inaugural competition had a mere eight entrants, the winner being Willie Park. But in the years that followed, it was opened up to players from every country, resulting in the world famous British Open we know today.

The Open was staged at Prestwick for its first twelve years, with "Old" Tom prevailing four times. His son, "Young" Tom, also won four titles, and by winning the competition three years in succession, claimed the belt by right. It was replaced in 1872 by the famous claret jug, which is still awarded to today's champion. The Open was last held at Prestwick in 1925, as the course had become unsuitable for accommodating the large number of spectators attending the annual event.

On the first hole, overlooking Links Road, is a four-square cairn commemorating the very first Open. Henry Cotton unveiled it in 1977. The 3rd hole is renowned for the Cardinal bunker, whereas the 17th has remained unchanged since "Old" Tom's day, its Sahara bunker being the final downfall of many a fine round!

Ayrshire Coast-Prestwick Esplanade

*Prestwick Esplanade, from Grangemuir Road
to the Salt Pan Houses and Maryborough*

Prestwick Esplanade is just over one mile in length and stretches south as far as Maryborough. A line of typical coastal resort houses overlooks the first stretch, but after Grangemuir Road the coast and the town are separated by Prestwick St Nicholas golf course. The clubhouse is located off the Esplanade and was erected in 1892 to plans by John Mercer. It is adorned with a sculpture by W.G. Stevenson depicting a golfer.

The Town Council created the Esplanade in 1908 after negotiations with the local landowners to acquire the coastal strip. A sea wall was put up and, in 1910, a pavilion seating 350 was erected south of Grangemuir Road. Here a variety of seaside shows and other entertainment was provided for many years. However, as with most pavilions, the decline in summer holidaymakers resulted in its closure. It is now a fitness club. Beyond this is the compound used by Prestwick Sailing Club, and their small yachts and dinghies are often seen sailing in the bay here.

The houses overlooking the Esplanade are not particularly old, but a few have been converted into hotels or guesthouses.

The Esplanade is a popular walk, the northern end being the busier, with children's play park and putting green, the southern end quieter. Approaching the modern houses at Maryborough the shore becomes rockier.

At the headland on St Nicholas Golf Course are two old cottages that predate the course by some time. These are known as Bellrock and Bentfield cottages, now adjoined by some modern luxury houses. Another building, known as Maryborough, stood to the north. Salt manufacturers formerly occupied these old cottages.

Still standing are the Salt Pan Houses at Maryborough. Erected around 1760, they are perhaps the best surviving examples in Scotland. There are two cottages that were built to either side

Salt Pan Houses

of an evaporation pond. The final stage was carried out on the ground floor of the cottages, where fires in the vaults got rid of the last of the water. External stairways led up to the salters' homes on the first floor.

The manufacture of salt has a long history in this locale, dating at least from 1470 when Thomas Crawford is noted as having pans hereabouts. In 1720 John Guthrie was the manufacturer at Bellrock cottage.

The trade was hard, and coals had to be transported from local pits to evaporate the water, leaving behind what was a rather poor quality product. The manufacturer even had to compete with salt smuggled in from Ireland, which evaded the tax payable on locally produced salt. Sometime between 1831 and 1841 the trade died out, unable to cope with the better quality imports.

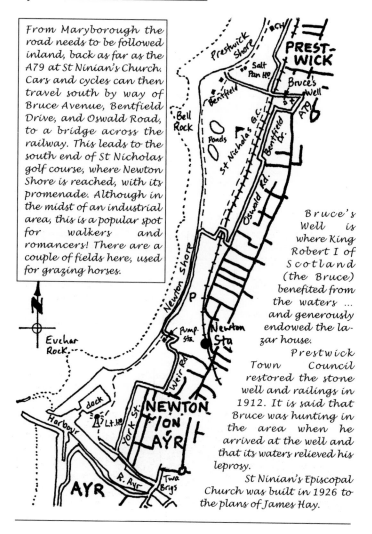

From Maryborough the road needs to be followed inland, back as far as the A79 at St Ninian's Church. Cars and cycles can then travel south by way of Bruce Avenue, Bentfield Drive, and Oswald Road, to a bridge across the railway. This leads to the south end of St Nicholas golf course, where Newton Shore is reached, with its promenade. Although in the midst of an industrial area, this is a popular spot for walkers and romancers! There are a couple of fields here, used for grazing horses.

Bruce's Well is where King Robert I of Scotland (the Bruce) benefited from the waters ... and generously endowed the lazar house.

Prestwick Town Council restored the stone well and railings in 1912. It is said that Bruce was hunting in the area when he arrived at the well and that its waters relieved his leprosy.

St Ninian's Episcopal Church was built in 1926 to the plans of James Hay.

A variety of routes can be followed from Newton promenade, through Newton upon Ayr, to the New Bridge over the River Ayr. For those on two wheels the cycle way is perhaps the easiest to follow, being marked on the ground and signposted. This makes its way directly down Weir Road and Peebles Street to Main Street and onto the New Bridge.

Pedestrians may wish to explore the triangle of land to the west of this, although it is an industrialised area. A roadway can be followed from Saltpans Road along the coast towards the headland at Euchar Rock. The road is then followed round Newton Dock, the main part of Ayr harbour.

Located on a site that somehow seems too far inland is Ayr lighthouse. This is a fairly typical structure, with a circular tower and adjoining lighthouse-keeper's cottage. The lighthouse was designed by Robert Paton and built in 1841. It still has its original wrought iron lantern, held together by rivets, and containing the original square-glass pieces. The keeper's cottage was added in 1850, the round kitchen being located on the ground floor of the tower.

North Harbour Street can then be followed upstream to the New Bridge. There are a few modern flats on the quayside, and at the junction with Main Street is the Border-line Theatre in the former Darlington Place Church of 1860.

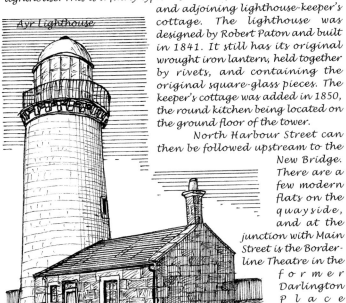

Ayr Lighthouse

Ayrshire Coast-Ayr-The Twa Brigs

The New Bridge was erected in 1878 to the plans of Blyth and Cunningham. It is the second bridge to occupy the site, as its 1786 predecessor collapsed in a storm. Robert Burns had prophesied this in his poem "The Brigs of Ayr", in which the former New Bridge and the existing Auld Brig argue between themselves. The Auld Brig tells the New Bridge that:

> "I'll be a brig when ye're a shapeless cairn."

The charming Auld Brig is well worth making a short detour to cross, as it is one of the oldest stone bridges in Scotland. The earliest reference to it dates from 1236 when King Alexander II granted a charter in favour of the burgesses of Ayr, to pay "for the maintenance of the bridge and the improvement of the harbour". The bridge was threatened with demolition at the beginning of the 20th century, but Burns enthusiasts campaigned for its restoration. Various plaques commemorating Burns and the restoration of 1907-10, as well as an old sundial, adorn it.

Downstream from the New Bridge, round sandstone pillars are visible on the river. These are all that remain of a railway bridge that once took a branch line to the southern harbour, from 1891 until the bridge was demolished in 1978.

Auld Brig

The south side of the harbour is no longer used to any great extent by boats. Until recently the fish market was located here, but was latterly moved to Troon. In its place modern flats have been constructed, lending this part of the town an attractive waterfront ambience.

On the river side of the street is a long, low sandstone building, now known as the Boathouse restaurant. Originally it was the local lifeboat station. On the landward side of the street

are a number of traditional dockside pubs, their names recalling the history of the immediate area, for example Ye Olde Forte Bar and the Steamboat Tavern.

Beyond are the public baths and the well-equipped leisure centre known as the Citadel. The street can be followed further west, eventually leading out onto the South Pier, terminated by a light beacon. At low tide the St Nicholas Rock can be seen in the bay, which has traditional connections with early Ayr.

Ayr harbour was at one time an important shipbuilding centre, but the last yard closed after the Second World War. From Sloan & Gemmell's yard the "Felix" was launched in 1850, for use by the intrepid Arctic explorer, Sir John Ross (1777-1856). The vessel was a 110-ton schooner and Ross often came to Ayr from his Stranraer home to supervise its construction.

Ayrshire Coast-Loudoun Hall

The oldest house in Ayr, Loudoun Hall is visible from South Harbour Street, where the road widens beyond Dante's bar. The lane here is known as the Boat Vennel, and at one time this was the main route from Ayr's High Street to the harbour. In the garden of the hall there are several interesting stone and metalwork sculptures, most of which have adopted a maritime theme.

Loudoun Hall itself is a three-storey building made of old local sandstone. It was probably built around 1513 by James Tait, provost of the burgh in 1521 and from 1527-9. However, it was

later owned by the Campbells of Loudoun Castle (near Galston) as their town house, this family being for years hereditary Sheriffs of Ayrshire. The Campbells owned the building until 1622, after which the status of the hall gradually declined over the decades until it was little more than a slum, divided into tiny flats.

The significance of the hall was spotted in the mid-20th century when the Marquis of Bute acquired it. He commissioned Robert Hurd to restore it between 1946-8. A more recent internal restoration has been undertaken.

The ground floor of the main block is vaulted, and the hall on the first floor has an impressive fireplace and aumbry.

The hall is used by a variety of local clubs and societies, and during the summer months is often home to an artist in residence, and other exhibitions. It is well worth a visit.

Miller's Folly

Oliver Cromwell created Ayr Citadel in 1652, at the time of the Commonwealth. A massive fort was constructed between the old town and the sea, guarding the harbour to its north. This had been the site of the former Ayr Castle. Walls were erected around the fort, revetted into the slope, and a moat was dug on the landward side, crossed by a bridge.

Inside this formidable redoubt were several barrack blocks, as well as other buildings required by a large complement of soldiers. These included a brewery, church, smithy, hospital, bake house, and stabling. Sentry posts were located at each corner along with a large gun emplacement at the north east corner, overlooking the harbour and town.

Within the fort the former parish church of St John was commandeered and its tower used as a lookout post. To compensate the parishioners Cromwell gifted a sum of money that helped to build the present old parish church, located off the High Street.

The fort was abandoned at the Restoration in 1680 and subsequently granted to the Earl of Eglinton in compensation for the losses he incurred during the time of the Protectorate.

Remains of the fort can still be seen on South Harbour Street, the Esplanade side and Cromwell Street. The original gateway to the fort remains "lost" in a narrow lane off Citadel Place, and St John's Tower survives in a small area of grassland.

The small turret overlooking the harbour is known as "Miller's Folly" after a local worthy, John Miller (1820-1910). He acquired most of the citadel lands and developed the present housing therein. He also incorporated the tower of St John into "Fort Castle", but this has since been restored to its original condition.

Ayrshire Coast-Ayr-Citadel Quay

The "Watchful" at Ayr's Citadel Quay

The western end of South Harbour Street has recently been developed as a desirable residential area, and a number of apartments have been built. Most of these have splendid views over the river, or across the bay to Arran.

The group of flats furthest west is known as Citadel Quay, and it overlooks the former slip of Ayr dockyard. The yard was established by the Harbour Trustees in 1881 and was operated for most of its life by Samuel MacKnight followed by Ailsa shipbuilders. Many ships were built there, the largest being the "Drake" of 1919, having a displacement of 1,597 tons. The yard was closed after the Second World War.

The former yard is now a feature on the shorefront. Within the slip is the "Watchful", an old fishing boat that was brought from the Maidens to Ayr, a simple reminder of Ayr's former association with fishing and boat building. Around the slip are a few sculptures, the largest being the chain and hook, perched on a boulder at the footbridge.

At the opposite side of the slip from Citadel Quay is the narrow access road to the South Pier, along which pedestrians an walk. This is 300 yards long and is terminated with a small light for guiding vessels.

From the South Pier, Ayr Esplanade stretches south for two miles alongside the glorious stretch of golden sands that forms Ayr beach. The local houses seem to turn their backs on the sea to start with, but in the early years there used to be a problem of blowing sands from the dunes that at one time occupied this area. However, in 1881 these were tamed with the construction of the first stretch of the Esplanade wall.

Half a mile from the harbour one reaches the County Buildings (1818) overlooking a small garden in which there is a memo-

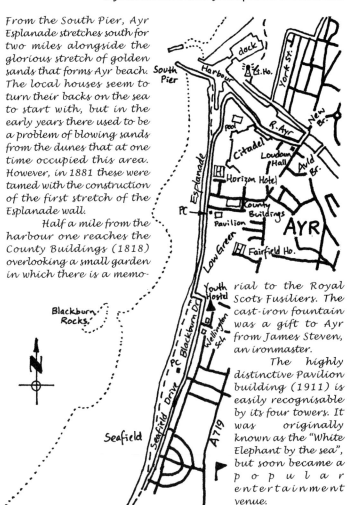

rial to the Royal Scots Fusiliers. The cast-iron fountain was a gift to Ayr from James Steven, an ironmaster.

The highly distinctive Pavilion building (1911) is easily recognisable by its four towers. It was originally known as the "White Elephant by the sea", but soon became a popular entertainment venue.

Ayrshire Coast-Ayr-The Low Green

South of the Pavilion is the impressive sward of grassland known as the Low Green. This is the only part of Ayr's former common lands still in existence, and it forms a welcoming open lung in the centre of town. The Low Green was part of an extensive tract of land, stretching from the town south to the River Doon, that was granted to the burgh by King William the Lion around 1205. A memorial at the north end of the Green, near to the Pavilion, commemorates the gift and gives details of the Low Green's long history.

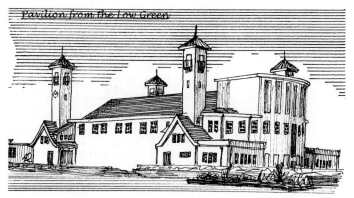

Pavilion from the Low Green

In the 19th century, various football and hockey clubs played here, but the council decided that these should be banned and the place left for picnickers and walkers. Today it is home to kite-fliers, dog-walkers, sun-worshippers and the odd unofficial football match.

At the end of the Second World War Billy Butlin wished to buy the Low Green and convert it into a large funfair and amusement park. The council voted against this, and Butlin developed the former HMS "Scotia" camp at the Heads of Ayr instead.

In front of the Pavilion is a large play park, popular with children at all times of the year. Toilets are located nearby, and there are a variety of fast food and ice cream outlets in the vicinity.

Carleton Turrets, now part of Wellington School

The public road strikes back from the Esplanade at the south end of the Low Green, but walkers and cyclists can continue along the top of the sea wall, overlooking the beach. Behind the roadway (Blackburn Road) are three large former houses, the most northerly being Craigweil, a Scottish Youth Hostel. Unfortunately this is the only Youth Hostel in Ayrshire. Craigweil is a baronial house of 1879 (by John Murdoch), built for John Sword, founder of the Western SMT bus company.

Next door to the hostel is Westfield and Carleton Turrets. These two houses now form part of Wellington School, a private establishment that has its origins in Wellington Square in 1839. Originally for girls only, the school has been co-educational since 1994.

At the foot of Seafield Road is a slip where a number of sailing boats and small yachts are launched. The Esplanade continues along the shore past the houses of Seafield to an open area around Cunning Park. The cycleway and path continue along the shore, crossing the Slaphouse Burn by a bridge and reaching the mouth of the River Doon.

A roadway can be followed up the side of the river to Doonfoot Bridge, where it meets the main A719. Here is Doonfoot Stores, a handy shop.

Ayrshire Coast-Doonfoot

On the right is Balgarth House Hotel, built in 1892 to the plans of the leading Ayr architect, James Morris (1852-1942). Those keeping as close to the coast as possible should strike north down Scaur o' Doon Road which is a hundred yards or so further on. This road terminates at the mouth of the river. A short walk across the grass brings one to Castle Walk, one side of which has private houses, the other being a grassy area on the shore. There are public toilets here. The way can then be made westward around Longhill Point towards Greenan Castle.

During the Second World War, Doonfoot was the site of a prisoner of war camp, which experienced the largest ever wartime escape in British history. In December 1944 these prisoners managed to make good their escape over the fence at the southern end of the camp. The authorities were slow in discovering the escape, but once they became aware of what had happened the emergency services sprang into action. Most of the prisoners were recaptured, some less than a mile away at Belleisle woods, where they had stopped to build a fire because of the cold! As late as 1948 one of the camp's residents went on hunger strike. Squatters later occupied the camp, a far cry from the present douce residents on the site!

From Greenan the cycle route heads across the fields past High Greenan to the A719 once more. This should then be followed west, past Craig Tara holiday park.

Doonfoot Stores

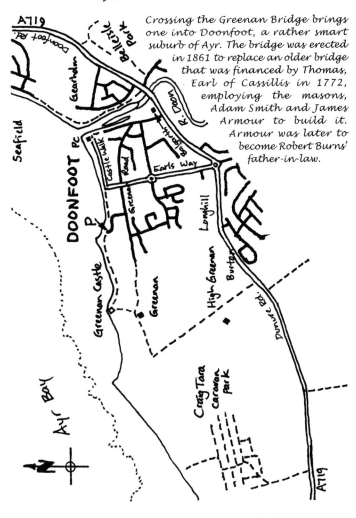

Crossing the Greenan Bridge brings one into Doonfoot, a rather smart suburb of Ayr. The bridge was erected in 1861 to replace an older bridge that was financed by Thomas, Earl of Cassillis in 1772, employing the masons, Adam Smith and James Armour to build it. Armour was later to become Robert Burns' father-in-law.

Ayrshire Coast-Greenan Castle

Greenan Castle is a smallish square-plan tower house, remarkable in its location - perched on a high cliff top that is slowly being eroded by the battering waves at its foot. Someday, and it will be a sad one, the remains of the tower will tumble onto the beach and nothing will remain of this distinctive structure.

The Kennedy family, to mark the northernmost limits of their "kingdom" of Carrick, and to send a warning to those who lived in the more peaceful countryside around Ayr, built the castle. A date on the castle reads 1603, but this probably commemorates the rebuilding of a more ancient structure, as on the landward side of the tower are fragments of old earthworks.

It is argued by some historians that the older castle was the site of one of King Arthur's Camelots. On a more historically accurate note Sir Thomas Kennedy, the son of the 3rd Earl of Cassillis spent his last night here in 1602 before being murdered by Mure of Auchendrane.

The 1603 rebuilding was probably the work of John Kennedy of Baltersan, who owned another tower house near Maybole. The entrance is located on the ground floor, at a narrow point of land between the tower and the cliff. This gives access to a spiral stair in the north corner of the tower. It is this corner of the building that has suffered most, the walls being thinner and the cliff so near.

Ayrshire Coast-Craig Tara and the Heads of Ayr

To most Ayrshire residents, Craig Tara holiday park is still known as Butlin's, for Billy Butlin acquired the site in 1947 and developed it into one of his distinctive holiday camps. This format survived until 1988 when it was renamed Wonderwest World. The site was later acquired by the Haven group which demolished the original chalets (created out of military buildings) and put static caravans in their place.

Prior to Butlin's ownership it was the site of HMS "Scotia", a Royal Navy training camp established in 1942. A memorial stone within the grounds commemorates those who served in the camp.

When Butlin's took over it became a popular and lively holiday destination, with swimming pool, theatre, railways, chairlift (taken from a disused mine) and revues. The camp even had its own railway station and, up until 1968, special holidaymakers' trains arrived from towns in England.

The Heads of Ayr are two tall, almost sheer, cliffs, rising 250 feet out of the sea and they form an impressive landmark. Little separates the cliffs, and the hill that forms the seaward part is known as Bower Hill. The western cliff had a prehistoric promontory fort located at its western end, which must have been a very airy site during its occupation.

On the southern slopes of the eastern cliff there was a chapel building, but this has long-since disappeared from view.

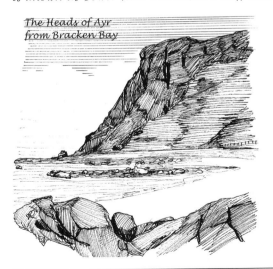

The Heads of Ayr from Bracken Bay

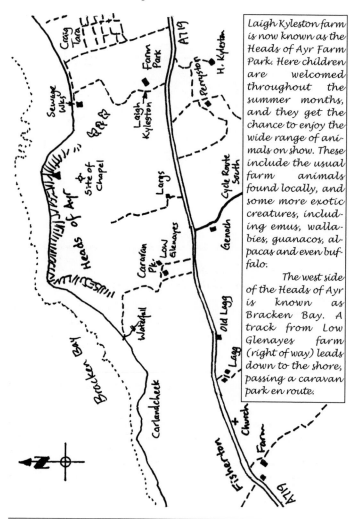

Laigh Kyleston farm is now known as the Heads of Ayr Farm Park. Here children are welcomed throughout the summer months, and they get the chance to enjoy the wide range of animals on show. These include the usual farm animals found locally, and some more exotic creatures, including emus, wallabies, guanacos, alpacas and even buffalo.

The west side of the Heads of Ayr is known as Bracken Bay. A track from Low Glenayes farm (right of way) leads down to the shore, passing a caravan park en route.

Fisherton Church

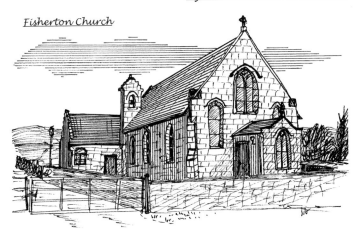

Fisherton is a hamlet located on the slopes of Drumbane, between the Heads of Ayr and Dunure, with which village it has many associations. On climbing the brae to Lagg farm, the first part of Fisherton encountered is the church. It was built in 1838, and altered in 1912.

Fisherton farm is next along the road, the largish house here being the manse. On the opposite side of the road a trackway leads down to Fisherton Cottage, built on a headland. The Drumbane Burn has waterfalls in its wooded gorge here, the last fall spilling over the cliff onto the shore.

Further along the main road, and fully one mile from the church, is Fisherton itself, complete with school. There was formerly a police station here.

On the hillside above Fisherton can be seen the tall tower of Dunduff Castle. The building of this L-planned tower began in the 16th century, but work was abandoned in 1696. The building lay in ruins for three centuries until the upper floors were completed and the building eventually occupied.

Near to the castle is a prehistoric fort, and further to the south-west are the scant ruins of the old church of Kirkbride in its small graveyard.

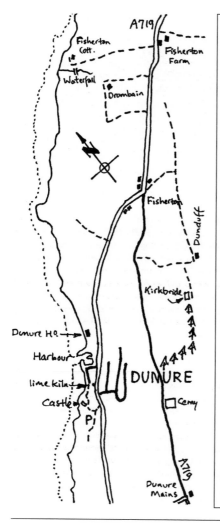

The A719 is followed round the western side of the Carrick Hills. The road sits on the hillside above the shore, the coastline being rather rocky in this part of the county. Nevertheless, it affords panoramic views down the Carrick shore and across the firth to Arran and Kintyre.

At Fisherton one should leave the main highway and follow the minor road that loops down to the picturesque village of Dunure. A visit is essential, for here can be seen a historic castle, quaint old houses around a tiny harbour, and a truly stunning stretch of coastline. Dunure is a justifiably popular spot for tourists, and there are a couple of tiny shops and a pub serving food.

The road climbs back up the hillside and rejoins the main road at Dunure Mains.

Dunure harbour

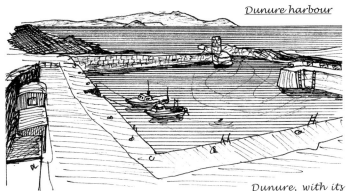

Dunure, with its spectacular location, is one of the most attractive villages on the Ayrshire coast. The tiny square harbour (rebuilt in 1811 at a cost of £50,000) is today home to tiny pleasure and fishing craft, but at one time it boasted a sizeable fishing fleet. Old sheds with nets and creels can be seen around it. The short pier leads to a much-eroded round tower.

Leases for ground were offered in 1819 where "a most advantageous fishing station and a place where various trades may be carried on, and a considerable intercourse by shipping may be established." However, these did not develop as anticipated.

Facing the harbour is a row of traditional houses, one of which is now the Anchorage Inn, and alongside is a small general store and a craft shop. Another row of houses is located at right angles behind this, and here is the Kennedy Hall of 1881. Pathways lead southward towards the doocot and castle. One of these passes the two old single-draw limekilns, which date from the early 19th century and a tearoom and ice cream shop is perched on top!

On the north side of the harbour a minor road passes in front of Dunure House (with its distinguished bow-front) before degenerating into a pathway along part of the shore. There are a number of headlands and cliffs beyond at Craiglowmount.

More modern houses are built in terraces above the old part of the village, where the Post Office can also be found.

The Limekilns, Dunure

The limekiln and doocot at Dunure are relics of a bygone age. Lime was in big demand for spreading on fields, used as an alkali against acidic soils. Doocots were the prerogative of the wealthy, for under Scots law one had to own a certain acreage to keep pigeons lawfully. These were kept for eating in the winter months, when the only alternative was salted beef and other meats. The doocot at Dunure is thought to date from the 16th century, and it is possible to go inside and see the many nesting holes.

The Doocot, Dunure

The castle at Dunure is one of the coast's most striking features. It stands a hoary ruin, perched on its cliff, and its history is one of bloodshed and torture.

The earliest reference to the lands occurs in 1256, since when it has been in Kennedy hands. One of its owners was Gilbert Kennedy, 4th Earl of Cassillis. He "was ane particuler manne, and ane werry greidy manne, and cairrit nocht how he gatt land, sa that he culd cum be the samin." It was he who mercilessly roasted the Commendator of Crossraguel Abbey in the castle's Black Vault in order to obtain the valuable lands associated with the abbey. So badly burned by the heat from the fire, the abbot was thereafter "onabill of his leggis". Lord Bargany, who also wished to acquire the lands, then besieged the castle.

Some of the walls of the castle are five feet thick. The oldest part is at the extreme tip of the promontory, where an irregular hexagonal block rises to a great height. The ground floor of this block was vaulted. The middle portion dates from the 15th century, whereas the most southerly part was built later. Fragments of old walls and earthworks are seen beyond the ruins.

The southern half of the castle was excavated in the 1990s and access is once again available to the public. Steel stairs allow access to the ruins, and information boards recount the castle's history. Further excavations are planned.

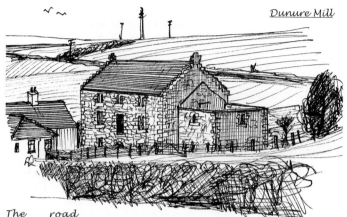

Dunure Mill

The road from Dunure rejoins the A719 at Dunure Mains, about half a mile from the village. On the way round a track leads down to an old lookout post above the Eggknock cliffs.

On the opposite side of the road from Mains farm is the disused Dunure Mill. The architecture of the mill building is rather distinctive, being somewhat ecclesiastical in appearance, and the building is adorned with crosses on the gables and twin and tripartite lancet windows. The mill workings were dismantled prior to 1948 and the millstones used for decorative purposes at Dunure Mains. In the early 19th century the miller was James Dow, a local poet of some repute.

Dunure Mains was the home of a famous Clydesdale horse known as "The Baron of Buchlyvie". The horse was born in 1903 and bred at Woodend farm in Buchlyvie, Stirlingshire, by William MacKeich. The joint owners of the horse fell out over it and the resultant case went as far as the House of Lords. The horse was put up for sale in 1911 and was purchased for a world record £9,500 by one of the disputers, William Dunlop of Dunure Mains. The horse died in 1914 from a kick. Initially buried at the farm, the skeleton was later disinterred and taken to Glasgow Art Gallery and Museum where it was on display for many years.

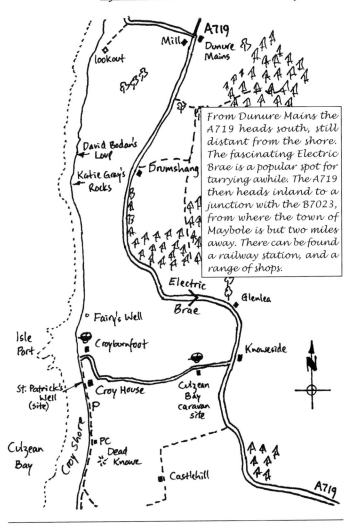

From Dunure Mains the A719 heads south, still distant from the shore. The fascinating Electric Brae is a popular spot for tarrying awhile. The A719 then heads inland to a junction with the B7023, from where the town of Maybole is but two miles away. There can be found a railway station, and a range of shops.

Ayrshire Coast-Croy Brae (Electric Brae)

The Croy Brae, situated on the road south from Dunure, is much better known as the "Electric Brae". Although there is no connection with electricity, the incline on the A719 is one of nature's mysteries, as stationary traffic on this section of road seems to be freewheeling uphill! While your mind insists that your car should be able to coast down the brae to the Craigencroy Glen, in fact it starts to go in the opposite direction. To experience the full effect, stop your car by the roadside and take the handbrake off.

The Electric Brae is, of course, a startling optical illusion. In reality, the road climbs from the "Ayr 9" milestone towards Craigencroy Glen. At the bridge, the road is 303 feet above sea level, whereas at the bend west of the milestone the road is only 286 feet above sea level. This gives the brae a gradient of 1 in 86. If you view the brae from the road to the south of Knoweside Farm the real direction of the gradient can be seen.

A granite boulder has been placed at the lay-by and the inscription explains how the illusion works. The Electric Brae has featured in countless newspaper articles, television programmes and books.

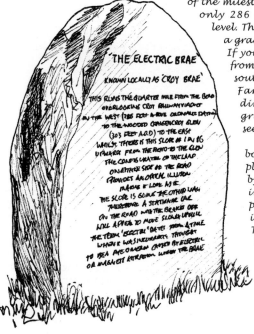

THE ELECTRIC BRAE

KNOWN LOCALLY AS 'CROY BRAE'

THIS RUNS THE QUARTER MILE FROM THE BEND OVERLOOKING CROY RAILWAY VIADUCT ON THE WEST (286 FEET ABOVE ORDNANCE DATUM) TO THE WOODED CRAIGENCROY GLEN (303 FEET A.O.D) TO THE EAST WHILST THERE IS THIS SLOPE OF 1 IN 86 UPWARD FROM THE ROAD TO THE GLEN THE CONFIGURATION OF THE LAND ON EITHER SIDE OF THE ROAD PROVIDES AN OPTICAL ILLUSION MAKING IT LOOK AS IF THE SLOPE IS GOING THE OTHER WAY THEREFORE A STATIONARY CAR ON THE ROAD WITH THE BRAKES OFF WILL APPEAR TO MOVE SLOWLY UPHILL THE TERM 'ELECTRIC' DATES FROM A TIME WHEN IT WAS INACCURATELY THOUGHT TO BE A PHENOMENON CAUSED BY ELECTRIC OR MAGNETIC ATTRACTION WITHIN THE BRAE

98

Croy Shore, or officially Culzean Bay, is one of Ayrshire's most popular and attractive beaches. From Knoweside farm, just south of the Electric Brae, a roadway drops down to the raised beach. It reaches the shore at Burnfoot, where the Craigencroy Burn meets the sea. A parking area is located south of Croy House. From here is a fine beach stretching two miles to Culzean Castle, visible on its headland. At Croy House (previously a hotel) was the ancient

Croy Shore, looking past
Croy House

St Patrick's Well. On the north side of the headland at Burnfoot is another old well, known as the Fairy's Well.

A path from Burnfoot heads south along the shore to Culzean. It passes Rancleugh Cottages, above which is the Dead Knowe, which is no doubt associated with local lore and legend. Goatsgreen Cottage is a reworking of an old traditional building, extended in the 1960s. This point of the beach is known locally as Maybole Shore (even although the town is four miles inland). Access is possible to this point by a roadway from Balchriston Lodge.

Beyond Goatsgreen the pathway follows the foot of the Swallow Craigs, rounding two headlands before ascending past the Gasworks Cottage to Culzean Castle. When the tide is in there is not much room between the cliffs and the sea, but when it is out there is a wide expanse of sand.

Culzean Castle from the Fountain Court

Culzean Castle is arguably the jewel-in-the-crown on the Ayrshire coast. Built between 1777-92, it is a magnificent country house perched on a cliff, and even the colour of sandstone used in its construction is attractive. The castle we see today is essentially the work of Robert Adam, one of the greatest Scottish architects, although the building was extended in Victorian times. Fortunately, however, the additions by Wardrop and Reid complement Adam's original design.

Robert Adam was asked by the 10th Earl of Cassillis to rebuild an old Scots tower house that stood on the cliff top at the southern end of Culzean Bay. The tower had been a Kennedy seat for centuries, and played its fair share in the troublesome quarrels that beset the family.

Adam's plan was to build to either side and behind the tower, refacing the front that was still visible, so that no sign of it remains today. It still exists internally, however, forming the Old Eating Room, Picture Room and rooms above.

The gothic castle is typical of Adam's castle style, but here it is at its most fully developed. He has even managed to adapt the building to its location, and a fine, circular bay projects onto the cliff head, affording panoramic views of the firth. Down below, Adam even had the old smugglers' caves reinforced to support the building.

Culzean Castle is now owned by the National Trust for Scotland and, with the country park, is its most popular visitor attraction.

Tours of the castle begin at the entrance hall, which is followed by the Armoury, decorated with a fine collection of swords and guns originally belonging to the West Lowland Fencibles. The Old Eating Room follows, occupying the original tower's ground floor. The Dining Room is next, after which visitors reach the magnificent Oval Staircase, one of Culzean's most outstanding features.

On the first floor is the Saloon, a circular room overlooking the firth. A suite of bedroom and dressing room follows, along with drawing rooms, an exhibition on General Dwight D Eisenhower and the Second World War, and the old kitchen.

Throughout the castle are fine examples of furniture, paintings, silverware, porcelain, plasterwork and the other accoutrements associated with a grand country house.

Most of the rooms have been restored to Adam's original plans, following careful investigation to find the old colour schemes. A comprehensive restoration programme is underway at Culzean, and invariably there is at least one part of the castle or policies being worked on. Quite often it is just as interesting to see this work progress.

Plan of first floor, Culzean Castle

Ayrshire Coast-Culzean Country Park

The policies of Culzean were established in 1969 as a country park (the first in Scotland), run by the Trust and the local council. The grounds are extensive (563 acres), and contain buildings of great architectural distinction, including the Viaduct, Camellia House, Gas House, Park Centre, Pagoda and Swan Pond cottage.

The grounds have a considerable number of pathways for walks, each having its own charm and distinctive atmosphere. One of the finest must be that which makes its way around the Swan Pond then along the wooded cliff-top towards the castle. Also worthy of note is the Vinery, a new building copied from the original structure of 1860.

The Park centre is located in what was Adam's Home Farm, a unique collection of buildings built

Culzean Home Farm

around a courtyard, which is accessed through large archways. Here can be found a restaurant, gift shop, visitor centre detailing the history of the estate and a stone barn, in which various exhibitions and events are held.

The Gas House is located by the side of the pathway down to the shore, and has an exhibition on William Murdoch (1754-1839), the Ayrshire-born inventor who did so much to promote the use of coal gas for lighting and other purposes.

Those more interested in gardens will enjoy the walled gardens and Fountain Court, which is terraced to the landward side of the castle and is home to palm and other exotic species. The parkland is worthy of more than one day, and the walker will be sorely tempted to linger awhile.

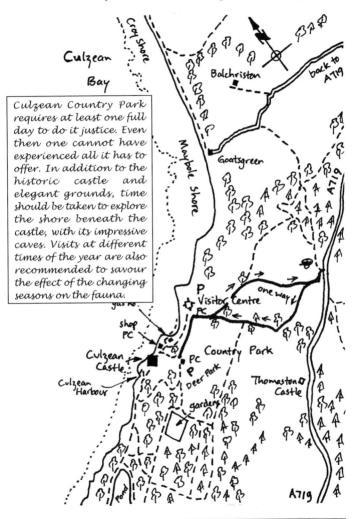

Culzean Bay

Balchriston

Croy Shore

Maybole Shore

back to A719

A719

Goatsgreen

Culzean Country Park requires at least one full day to do it justice. Even then one cannot have experienced all it has to offer. In addition to the historic castle and elegant grounds, time should be taken to explore the shore beneath the castle, with its impressive caves. Visits at different times of the year are also recommended to savour the effect of the changing seasons on the fauna.

gas ho

P
Visitor Centre
PC
one way

shop
PC

Culzean Castle

Culzean Harbour

PC Country Park

P
Deer Park

gardens

Thomaston Castle

pond

A719

Ayrshire Coast-Culzean Harbour

On the shore immediately west of Culzean Castle is a small sandy bay known as Culzean Harbour. From the West Battery (with its cannon) a zigzag pathway drops to the shore, where a large wooden boat-shed is located. On the water's side is a roughly built stone wharf.

Perhaps surprisingly, this was the location for a shipbuilding enterprise. The 3rd Marquis of Ailsa was a keen seaman and he established a yard at the Maidens. At times of peak demand he used Culzean for additional work. The Marquis built a number of vessels here but when the business expanded he moved to a new yard at Troon, where the Ailsa Shipbuilding Company was to operate for many years. In later years the boathouse was used to store a 12-oar lifeboat, manned by employees on the estate.

Culzean Harbour-the boatshed below the castle viewed from the old wharf

There are a few other buildings situated on the shore. These include the Dolphin House (built by Adam as a laundry and typical of the Culzean style), and a cylindrical bathing house. The Dolphin House is now an outdoor centre and the modern timber building adjoining is for accommodation.

The headland known as Barwhin Point is located at the north end of Maidenhead Bay. There is a long-standing tradition that it took its name from the time when Robert the Bruce was hiding on Arran. He sent a supporter to the Carrick shore to see if the folk were ready to rally behind him. If they were, he was told to light a beacon so that Bruce could bring his small band of warriors across and begin his campaign. The soldier landed, but finding the area full of English soldiers decided against lighting the fire. Unfortunately, one of the locals was burning whin bushes at this very spot, and the Bruce misread the flames as an invitation to land. Finding the countryside overrun by the enemy, he headed for the Galloway Hills from where he prosecuted his successful guerrilla campaign.

Immediately to the north of Barwhin Point is a small and secluded sandy bay, accessible from Culzean's policies.

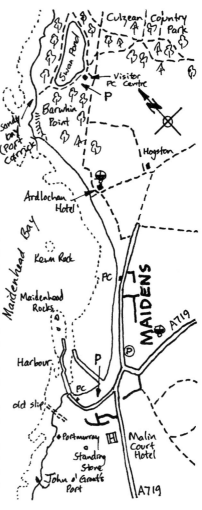

Ayrshire Coast-Maidens

Maidens harbour

The Maidens, as the locals call the village, is located on the north side of Turnberry Point, overlooking Maidenhead Bay. This delightful village probably got its name from the Maidenhead Rocks, which lie at the end of the long pier and breakwater that protects the little sandy harbour. It was at one time a busy fishing port, but today is home to just a few pleasure craft. The harbour dates from the 18th century. To the west of the low headland, where the nets were formerly dried and cleaned, is a disused slipway associated with the boat building firm of Alexander MacCredie, established in 1883 to build steamers.

Beyond the slipway is Port Murray, a small sandy bay between rocks, overlooked by a prize-winning "modern" house of 1963, designed by Peter Womersley. A second beach is a few hundred yards further west, known as John o' Groat's Port. Hereabouts are a few rocky cliffs, part of Bain's Hill, which has a prehistoric standing stone perched near its summit. Just inland from the Maidens is Shanter farm, original home of Burns' "Tam o' Shanter".

It is possible to walk from the Culzean policies down to the shore at Barwhin Point, either to the north or south of the headland, and then make your way past Ardlochan House and Ardlochan Hotel and a caravan park, to the first row of bungalows in Maidens. The main buildings of note are the former church hall and the Bruce Hotel, with its sculpture depicting Bruce and the Spider, by Bruce Weir.

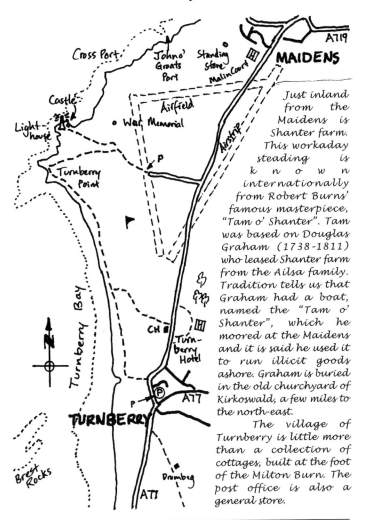

Just inland from the Maidens is Shanter farm. This workaday steading is known internationally from Robert Burns' famous masterpiece, "Tam o' Shanter". Tam was based on Douglas Graham (1738-1811) who leased Shanter farm from the Ailsa family. Tradition tells us that Graham had a boat, named the "Tam o' Shanter", which he moored at the Maidens and it is said he used it to run illicit goods ashore. Graham is buried in the old churchyard of Kirkoswald, a few miles to the north-east.

The village of Turnberry is little more than a collection of cottages, built at the foot of the Milton Burn. The post office is also a general store.

Turnberry Point is the location of Turnberry Lighthouse, which itself occupies much of the site of Turnberry Castle. A right of way to the point leads across the golf course, leaving the A719 half a mile south of the Maidens. A small parking area is formed where the roadway crosses the former airfield runway.

Turnberry Castle is today little more than a fragmentary ruin. Only the roughest of masonry can be seen, most of it long-since destroyed by erosion and redevelopment. The biggest part is located on a cliff to the north of the lighthouse.

Many historians believe that Robert the Bruce, the victor of Bannockburn, was born here in 1274, though Dumfriesshire folk claim Lochmaben Castle as his birthplace. The story goes that the dowager Countess of Carrick took a fancy to one of Lord Annandale's sons and had him kidnapped. Back at Turnberry he gradually succumbed to her charms and they were married in 1271. Three years later the great Scots hero, and future King, was born.

Turnberry Lighthouse was erected in 1873 to the designs of Thomas Stevenson, father of Robert Louis Stevenson. It is a brick-built structure, and is now fully automated. The old walled garden still survives, and at the far end of the point a broken pathway drops down to a small quay among the rocks.

The landing strip at Turnberry occupies part of a wartime aerodrome, established in 1917 for the School of Aerial Gunnery. An 'A'-shaped 'drome, the runways were 2,010, 1,400 and 1,250 yards in length, each 50 yards wide. Although these were big enough, the airfield had limited hard standing for aircraft. Within Tauchet Wood, behind Turnberry Hotel, can be found remains of the original bomb stores.

The dead who served here are commemorated on a war memorial. This is situated on a low knoll, near to Turnberry Lighthouse, and lists airmen from Britain, America and Australia. The tall white granite cross, designed by Col. Hugh Wallace of Busby, was unveiled in May 1923 by the Marquis of Ailsa. It reads:

"To the officers, non-commissioned officers, and men of the Royal Flying Corps, Royal Air Force, and Australian and United States Air Services who gave their lives for their country while serving in the School of Aerial Gunnery & Fighting at Turnberry, MCMXVII-MCMXVIII. Their names liveth for evermore."

The names and ranks of 39 servicemen are listed on the other three sides of the memorial which, when erected, was the only tribute of its kind to the RAF.

During the Second World War, the airfield was used by the Coastal Command as an operational training unit. At one time there were 2345 RAF personnel based here, in addition to 437 WAAF personnel. The base closed in 1945 and the main buildings, including five hangars, were demolished.

Turnberry War Memorial

Ayrshire Coast-Turnberry Hotel and Golf Course

An elegant and impressive building, Turnberry is without doubt one of the world's great hotels. Established in 1904 by the Glasgow and South Western Railway company, the hotel was quick to gain an international reputation. It has a long, white facade and a jaunty red roof, and was designed by James Miller. At one time trains stopped at the front door, but the railway disappeared in 1942 and since 1983 the railway companies have not owned it.

The land to the west of the hotel is occupied by two championship golf courses - the Ailsa and the Kintyre. Mackenzie

Turnberry Hotel

Ross designed the Ailsa course in the 1950s, and its 9th hole - known as Bruce's Castle - has one of the most spectacular tees in world golf, perched on a rock. The course is 6,976 yards long and a par 69. Donald Steel designed the Kintyre course in the 1990s, replacing the old Arran course. Eleven of the holes were totally redesigned to create a magnificent links course 6,827 yards in length. This course is a par 72.

The first Open Championship to be held at Turnberry was in 1977, when Tom Watson beat Jack Nicklaus in one of the most thrilling tournaments in history. Opens were also staged here in 1986 (won by Greg Norman) and 1994 (Nick Price). The Duke of York opened the new clubhouse in 1993 and here too is the Colin Montgomerie Links Golf Academy.

Heading south from Turnberry village the A77 wends its way along the raised beach, home to innumerable potato fields. Each year, from these fields, the first crop of the famous Ayrshire "tatties" is collected. Their early harvest is greatly assisted by the proximity to the coast, which is warmed by the Gulf Stream.

Balkenna has a café where meals are available. Balkenna Hill, which is only 175 feet high, has a small mound near its summit known as the Fairy Knowe, the history of which is unknown.

To the south of this is Dowhill Farm, where a farm shop sells locally grown produce. The earthworks on the Dowhill Mount (immediately to the south) have a more historic origin. Here stood an early motte hill with defensive ditches on the landward side. On the highest point of the motte can be seen a circular ring of stones, which may have been the masonry base of a wooden castle (a most unusual survivor) or else a stone-built dun.

A large seaweed factory, established in 1934, occupies the raised beach at Dipple. Here kelp and other brown seaweed which has been harvested all over Scotland (as far away as the Hebrides) is processed into alginates, much used in the food, drinks, paper and pharmaceutical industries. The factory was operated by Alginate Industries Limited, which in 1979 merged with Kelco International of California.

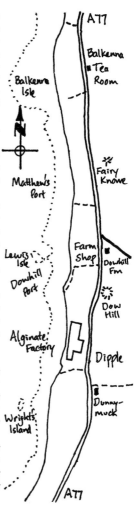

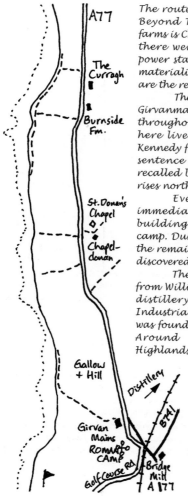

The route south follows the busy A77. Beyond The Curragh and Burnside farms is Chapeldonan farm. At one time there were plans to erect a nuclear power station here, but these did not materialise. Just north of the steading are the remnants of St Donan's Chapel.

The name Girvan Mains (usually Girvanmains) is one that is well known throughout the history of Carrick, for here lived a notable branch of the Kennedy family. The chieftain's right to sentence reprobates to be hanged is recalled by the low Gallow Hill, which rises north of the farm.

Even earlier, the ground immediately south of the farm buildings was the site of a Roman camp. During road realignment work the remains of a marching camp were discovered.

The smell hereabouts emanates from William Grant and Sons' whisky distillery, located in Grangestone Industrial Estate. The grain distillery was founded in 1964 to produce spirit. Around twenty malts from the Highlands are blended with the grain spirit to produce Grant's "Standfast" blended whisky.

Those who wish to keep closer to the coast (and get away from the A77 for a while) should turn off at Girvan Mains and follow Golf Course Road through the middle of the course to Newton Kennedy.

Golf Course Road should be followed from Girvan Mains through the middle of Girvan golf course to a line of houses located on a spit of land between the sea and the Water of Girvan. Beyond is part of Girvan known as Newton Kennedy, for here in the 18th century Kennedy of Dunure established a small village that he hoped would rival the larger town to the south.

At the southernmost point of Newton Kennedy is Noble's shipbuilding yard, where fishing boats are made, repaired or repainted. Here also is the clubhouse of the Carrick Sailing Club and the local Coastguard offices.

The MacCreath Park lies between Newton Kennedy houses and the shore. From here a walk over the low hill (78 feet!) known as Knockavalley can be made.

A bridge crosses the river from Newton Kennedy to Girvan. Just east of where the road joins the A77 one can see the old cemetery of the town, reached through a large triumphal archway, erected in memory of William Johnstone and designed by James Morris in 1908. Here one can find the grave of Alexander Ross, a special constable, shot on 12 July 1831 at the Sheddings during an Orange march. His killer was later hanged in Ayr and a memorial marks where he died. The old parish church used to be located in this cemetery, where some old graveslabs can be seen.

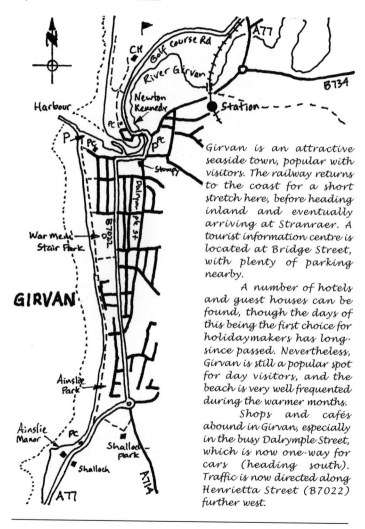

Girvan is an attractive seaside town, popular with visitors. The railway returns to the coast for a short stretch here, before heading inland and eventually arriving at Stranraer. A tourist information centre is located at Bridge Street, with plenty of parking nearby.

A number of hotels and guest houses can be found, though the days of this being the first choice for holidaymakers has long-since passed. Nevertheless, Girvan is still a popular spot for day visitors, and the beach is very well frequented during the warmer months.

Shops and cafés abound in Girvan, especially in the busy Dalrymple Street, which is now one-way for cars (heading south). Traffic is now directed along Henrietta Street (B7022) further west.

Girvan is really quite an old town, but there is nothing of any great age surviving, as most of the town was redeveloped in the 19th century. The main part of the burgh follows a grid pattern, and was developed as a holiday resort in the 20th century. Today the beach no longer has the same attraction for summer vacations, but it is still very popular with day-trippers.

In the centre of the town, at the cross, is the "Old Stumpy" steeple, the only survivor of the old town house. The steeple dates from the 18th century, but its surrounding buildings were demolished in 1956 following a fire in 1939.

South of this is the main shopping area, Dalrymple Street, where the MacKechnie Institute, a local museum and exhibition area, is also located.

The oldest part of the town was situated to the north of the cross, but nothing of any great antiquity survives. Here is a large car park, tourist information centre, toilets, renowned chip shop and ice cream salesmen, and the former "High Street", now little more than a pedestrian path! At the end of Vicarton Street, which is lined with double-storey terraced homes, is the railway station.

In earlier centuries, Girvan was a thriving port, exporting coal from the Dailly coalfield, and landing fish caught all over the west coast. The harbour was rebuilt in 1824 when quays were created along the side of the river, and again in 1869. The pier dates from 1881. At one time pleasure steamers made Girvan one of their principal stops, but today it is more likely to be yachts that land, a new jetty having been added to allow them to moor.

Ayrshire Coast-Girvan Harbour

From Girvan cross, one should follow Knockcushan Street in a westerly direction towards the harbour. Within a short distance, on the left, are the gates to Knockcushan Gardens. Here is a small aviary and a memorial commemorating the fact that this was the original site of Girvan's seat of justice, where Robert the Bruce is supposed to have held court in 1328.

The opposite side of the street has no buildings, the ground d r o p p i n g steeply to the w a t e r s i d e, where a harbour has been formed in the mouth of the river. A small jetty bends out into the river, protecting the small pleasure craft and fishing boats that make this their base. Fishing and pleasure trips can also be arranged here and the harbour is home to a modern lifeboat station.

The shore hereabouts is home to a variety of attractions, popular with summer tourists. There are several amusement arcades, as well as the swimming pool and pavilion of 1972, which have toilets and a large parking area. The modern looking building is a sewage pumping station, erected in the 1990s. It is adorned with aquatic carvings. A granite memorial fountain is located nearby.

At the west end of the harbour is a coastguard station, located at the landward end of the pier. This projects out into the sea for 600 yards and has a light beacon at its extremity.

Boats from Girvan harbour offer pleasure and fishing trips to the fascinating island of Ailsa Craig. These can be booked by telephoning one of the numbers on the boards at the harbour side. The island is located ten miles to the west of Girvan, and an excursion takes several hours.

Ailsa Craig, or "Paddy's Milestone" as it is nicknamed, is a massive granite rock boss, rising 1,110 feet out of the firth. One of the cliffs, the imposing Barestack, is 625 feet tall, making it one of the biggest in Britain. There are few areas of level ground on the island, and these are confined to the east side, where a lighthouse (1883-6, by D & T Stevenson) stands 35 feet in height, automatic since 1990. On the triangular area of grass and stones there are, perhaps surprisingly, a gasworks, railway lines and other relics of the thriving quarry that was once located here. The stone was, and still is, in demand for making curling stones, the fine granite being ideal for skimming across the ice.

Also on the island, high above the lighthouse, stands the simple rectangular keep of Ailsa Craig Castle. Thomas Hamilton who was appointed the keeper of the island erected this in 1597.

The keep is vaulted on the ground and first floors. The first floor contains a large fireplace and two smallish apartments. From here a spiral stairway led up to the second floor, now ruinous, but which may have contained sleeping accommodation. On the hillside above the tower is the Castle Well. According to MacGibbon and Ross's guide to the castles of Scotland, the castle "must have been the fortress of a pirate chief, who issued from it to plunder the surrounding seas and coast, for the island would never yield the sustenance necessary for the captain and crew."

Ailsa Craig Castle

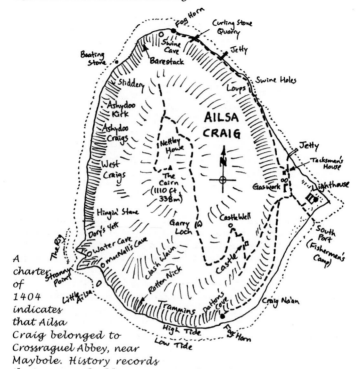

A charter of 1404 indicates that Ailsa Craig belonged to Crossraguel Abbey, near Maybole. History records that wayward abbots were sent here for a spell of solitary confinement. At the time of the Reformation, Ailsa Craig was annexed by Hew Barclay of Ladyland for Philip of Spain, but he was quickly ejected. Since 1560 the Kennedy family, whose chief takes his title, Marquis of Ailsa, from it, has owned the island.

Ailsa Craig is a Site of Special Scientific Interest, where gannets and other seabirds are left undisturbed. This is in stark contrast to the Victorian era, during which steamers were wont to sail alongside and blast their horns, frightening the birds into flight and creating a "wonderfully sublime" scene, according to an old guide.

_Woodland Bay from the Black
Neuk, looking towards Shalloch_

The sea front at Girvan is a popular spot for holidaymakers and picnickers during the summer months. Girvan has a mile and a half of golden sands stretching south from the harbour. A pathway makes its way along the promenade for the full length, rejoining the A77 at Shalloch, to the south of the town.

At the parking area next to the harbour is a granite memorial fountain erected in 1927 to the memory of Captain Alexander Clachar and his wife. The first stretch of the green is occupied by the boating pond and swing park. Originally designed in something akin to the "Willow Pattern", it was the work of James Wright, a noted Scottish artist. Beyond this is an open stretch of grass, backed by a line of houses.

Stair Park follows, a wide expanse of grassland. Here is a memorial to the dead of two world wars. The pavilion at the southern end has public toilets.

A cemetery is located at the southern end of the park. Beyond, the houses are much closer to the sea wall, and continue as far as Shalloch and Ainslie Manor nursing home. Another open stretch of grassland here is known as Ainslie Park. On the shorefront here is a car park, picnic area, toilets, and often a fast-food caravan.

Just beyond this is Shalloch Mill, long-since disused as a working mill, followed by Woodland farm and its sandy bay.

The Carrick shore is renowned for its geological formation. Here is the western end of the Southern Upland boundary fault, which separates the central lowlands from the uplands of the south. At the western end the line of the fault is obscure, but it was responsible for some rather fine features in the landscape, notably the straight line of Glen App.

At Craigskelly, near Shalloch, the conglomerates and flagstones and schists meet in a rather fine way. According to the noted geologist, Sir Roderick Murchison, the rocks at Kennedy's pass are "by far the finest example of coarse Silurian conglomerates I have met with in any part of the world."

Most of the coast from Girvan to Glen App has rocks of the Ordovician period, the volcanic rocks containing graptolite shales, cherts, and serpentinite intrusions. Semi precious stones such as red jasper and white quartz can be found on the shores. Some of the cliffs show isoclinal folding, that is beds of rock that have been folded over.

At Downan Point, south of Ballantrae, can be seen some rather fine pillow-lavas, formed when lava erupted beneath the sea, resulting in a rapid cooling effect. The resultant rock - spilite - is a type of basalt rich in soda, and is distinguished by its likeness to large globules like pillows.

Beyond the Black Neuk, where the main road takes a sharp bend, one reaches the gatehouse at Ardmillan which has been restored and marks the entrance to Ardmillan Caravan Site. This occupies the grounds of Ardmillan Castle, which was destroyed by fire in 1972, killing the lady owner. The ruins stood here until 1991 when they were demolished.

Ardmillan was of course a Kennedy seat, being built in the late 16th century. In 1656 the estate passed to Craufurd hands following the marriage of the heiress, Marion, to James Craufurd of Baidland. The Craufurd laird was a noted persecutor of the Covenanters. The Craufurds extended the building with the addition of a Georgian wing, which was said to have contained one of the most elegant drawing rooms in the county. Later owners included Patrick Playfair.

One of the more famous occupants of the castle was James Craufurd, Lord Ardmillan (1805-76). Born in Hampshire, he was educated in Ayr and Edinburgh. In 1855 he was appointed a lord of the Court of Session. Probably his most famous decision was made in the Yelverton case.

On the slopes of the Byne Hill above the castle stands an old memorial to Archibald Clifford Blackwell Craufurd, Lord Ardmillan's father, but this no longer bears any inscription. He served in the army in India and took part in the capture of the Cape of Good Hope in 1795. His wife was also renowned locally for her benefactions, making gifts to the poor of Girvan and other good deeds.

Ardmillan Castle in its heyday

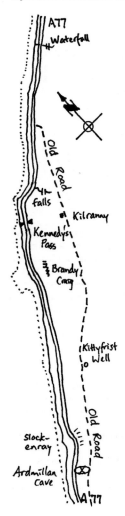

Just beyond Ardwell Point the main road has to force its way between the sea and cliffs at a spot known as Kennedy's Pass. At one time the road was much narrower here, having to pass between narrow rocks, but blasting over the years has gradually widened the gap, allowing the traffic to pass through unhindered. Today there is only one finger of rock blocking the seaward side, often painted with a message such as "Christ died for our sins".

The Kennedy for whom the pass is named is the Right Hon. T.F. Kennedy of Dalquharran. In 1831 he was the first to use this narrow way as the route south when the pass opened. The roadway previously passed along the hillside above, and survives today as farm tracks. From the Kilranny Bridge the old road can be followed uphill to Kilranny farm, from where it keeps a fairly level route along the side of Pinbain Hill. On the side of the hill is the Kittyfrist Well, a spring where travellers were wont to slake their thirst. The old road drops down to the north end of Lendalfoot bay at Pinbain Bridge.

This part of the coast was ideal for smuggling illicit goods ashore, and the Brandy Craig just south of Kennedy's Pass recalls one of the contraband commodities landed hereabouts.

On the shore side of the A77, 450 yards or so north of Lendalfoot Bridge, is a small white-painted stone enclosure in which stands a sandstone memorial. It was "Erected to the memory of Archibald Hamilton and crew, natives of King's Cross, Arran, who were drowned near this place, September 11th 1731. Ye passengers who-er ye are, as ye pass on this way, disturb ye not this small respect, that's paid to sailors' clay". The present memorial dates from 1870 and replaces an older memorial, itself a replacement for the original. In 1885 a storm washed away part of the shore here, unearthing the bodies of Hamilton and his crew.

Nothing is known of the story of Archibald Hamilton and his crew who drowned off the Carrick shore, other than that which is recorded on the memorial. "Lloyd's Register and Shipping Gazette" was not published until 1734 and even well into the 19th century is very incomplete on lesser vessels, which this undoubtedly would have been.

In 1711 Kingscross was little more than a clachan, and there would probably not even have been a pier there. Boats belonging to the area would be drawn up the shingle beach in the lea of Kingscross Point.

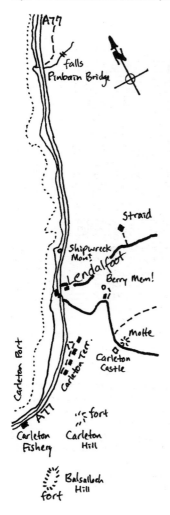

Lendalfoot, as its name suggests, is a hamlet located at the foot of the Lendal Water. A popular holiday destination, it has an outdoor centre, and a long row of holiday cottages (Carleton Terrace) at the foot of Carleton Hill. The oldest cottages were erected from around 1933 when the Hamilton estate offered feus.

At the west end of Carleton Bay is Carleton Fishery, which is dated 1832. On the beach here the sailing ship used in the 1970s television programme "The Onedin Line" ran aground, but its owners managed to refloat it.

Beyond the picnic area one comes to The Whilk, another spot occupied by holiday homes, huts and caravans. Some of these have been positioned around the rocks of the raised beach to afford some protection. The Whilk is the name of one of the older cottages here, a simple but-and-ben.

Further along the coast is the static caravan site at Bennane Shore, occupying the narrow grass space to either side of the old road.

Towering over the Carleton cottages are Carleton and Balsalloch hills, rising steeply from the shore. Both are crowned with ancient forts.

Carleton Castle from the west

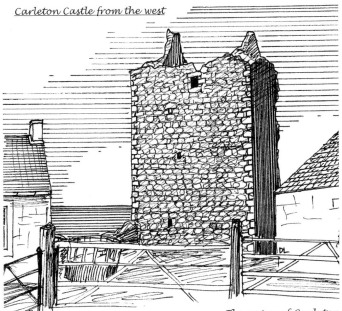

The ruins of Carleton
Castle stand by the side of Little Carleton farm, half a
mile up the Colmonell road from Lendalfoot. The remains
consist of a square tower, one corner of which has been removed
and a thinner wall erected in its place. The original stairway was
located within the thickness of the south east corner of the castle.
The castle originally had two vaults, over the basement and great
hall, but these have long-since disappeared. A service stair
linking the upper floors still survives in the tower.

Carleton was for many years a property of the Cathcart
family, and the tower may date from sometime in the 15th
century.

On the opposite side of the road from the castle can be seen
a Norman motte hill. The remains of another castle exist at
Knockdaw.

Ayrshire Coast-Charles Berry's Memorial

By the banks of the Lendal Water, a few hundred yards up the Colmonell road from the old school, stands an obelisk commemorating Charles Berry. It reads:

> Erected by a number of friends to the memory of Charles Berry who died at Lendalfoot, Feby. 1st 1909 aged 36 years, and was interred in Colmonell churchyard. He was widely known as a devoted ornithologist, botanist and geologist. "Great Nature Spoke, observant man obeyed."

Charles Berry was born in 1872, the son of a crofter from Lendalfoot. He later lived alone in a but-and-ben there, earning his living from fishing for shellfish, lobsters and crabs. He was a devoted naturalist, and he was invariably the first person in Scotland to report the arrival of the wheatear, the earliest migrant to Scotland. Through observation, he reckoned that the bird usually arrived on 20 March, and on that day he went to a spot on the shore known as The Whilk, ready to spot it.

Berry's cottage was a veritable museum of natural artefacts, which included semi-precious stones, fossils, minerals, birds' eggs and a huge collection of stuffed animals and birds. In one glass case was a model tree on which was mounted no fewer than 123 birds. Berry's gravestone in Colmonell churchyard is ornamented with carvings of a tree and a bird's nest.

When Berry died a friend was present. He recorded the great man's last words as he gazed over Lendalfoot shore, "If the other world be but as half as bonnie as this, I'll willingly gang awa'. Oh, man, it is a bonnie world."

Wheatear

At the west end of the Bennane Shore is a cliff known as the Games Loup. This is associated with the tale of the False Sir John Cathcart of Carleton. He was in the habit of marrying heiresses, their lack of beauty notwithstanding. Soon after the wedding, and once their estates had passed into to his hands, his wives mysteriously disappeared, never to be seen again. This seems to have continued for seven wives, until the eighth, May Collean (or Culzean), discovered his dastardly plan.

Sir John had been taking his new wife for a walk along the shore to the Games Loup, where he had thrown her predecessors over the cliff to their deaths. But when he tried the same trick with the redoubtable May, he met his match. She persuaded him to turn away whilst she took off her clothes, whereupon she pushed him over the rocks. An old ballad recounts the tale:

"Light down, light down," says fause Sir John,
"Your bridal bed you see;
Here have I drowned seven ladies fair,
The eighth one you shall be."

— — —

He turned himself straight round about
To look to the leaf o' the tree;
She has twined her arms around his waist,
And thrown him into the sea.

127

Ayrshire Coast-Sawney Bean's Cave

There is a lay-by at the side of the A77 at the top of the brae rising above Bennane Shore caravan site. From here a pathway zigzags down the face of the steep cliff to Balcreuchan Port, a small stony bay between high cliffs. At the north end of the bay there is a large cavern, known locally as Sawney Bean's cave.

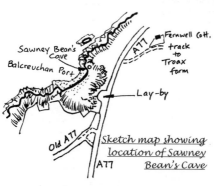

Sawney Bean (or Alexander or Samuel Bain or MacBain, depending on which account is read) is a legendary character in Carrick and Galloway lore. Some say he was a real-life character, but there are no official records of him having existed.

Sketch map showing location of Sawney Bean's Cave

Reputedly, Sawney Bean lived in this cave with his extended family. They had separated themselves from society and over the years found that they could survive alone. However, the cannibal clan had discovered a plentiful source of food - the innocent travellers making their way along this lonely stretch of coast. Coming at them from behind, they mercilessly strangled their victims before dragging them down the cliff to their lair.

Over a period of years the locals could not understand why so many travellers had disappeared, and assumed they had perished by falling over the cliffs. However, one of the ambushed men managed to make good his escape, and quickly raised the alarm. Soldiers were immediately sent to the area and carried out a thorough search, before they discovered the subterranean chamber down by the sea. Their gruesome findings included the remains of human skeletons, and a selection of limbs hanging from the ceiling, ready for the next meal. Legend has it that Sawney Bean and his family were all captured and hanged.

S.R. Crockett used the tale in his marvellous novel, "The Grey Man", one of the finest stories set in Carrick.

The A77 strikes inland at Balcreuchan Port and crosses Bennane Hill before dropping steeply to Bennane Lea. Bennane Hill is crowned by a prehistoric enclosure. Other historic mounds can be seen at Little Bennane, their origins obscure.

The present road replaces an older road that makes its way around Bennane Head. However, due to its proximity to the sea and the steepness of the cliffs, this road was often closed due to landslips and rock falls, resulting in a lengthy detour. It is possible to follow the route on foot, passing the tiny cove of Port Vad and the Bennane Cave.

Bennane Cave is walled off across its front, an old sandstone wall having been erected sometime in the 19th century. In the wall was a doorway (still extant) and a low window (now walled up). The area behind the wall is rather damp, drips of water constantly falling from the open cliff above, but further in it is drier, and no doubt has been utilised by man for many centuries.

The cave was for many years home to a number of tramps, the most recent being Henry Torbet, or "Snib" as he was known. The cave was at one time so well known that Alexander Henderson of Maybole published a postcard depicting it sometime in the early 20th century.

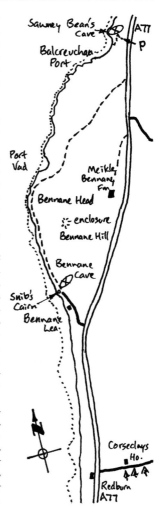

Ayrshire Coast-Snib's Cairn

At Bennane Head is a small cairn standing by the roadside, about 600 yards north of Bennane Lea. The cairn has a simple inscription: "Henry Ewing Torbet (Snib) of Bennane Cave 1912-1983. Respected and Independent".

Henry Torbet was a native of Dundee where he worked as a bank clerk until his 48th birthday in 1960. Around that time he decided to leave his job, friends and family to start a new life. He became a tramp, and journeyed all over Scotland, earning his keep by working on farms. At length he arrived in Carrick, where he found a rather good cave at Bennane Head which would become his home for the next 20 years. This he furnished with items found on his travels, or else with things he received in return for a day's work.

Gradually locals came to respect the old man and, as they did not know his real name, called him Snib after another tramp who used to frequent the cave in the 1920s. When asked his name he would reply, "They call me Snib Scott."

Although Snib received many gifts from the locals, he refused to accept cash, even when he was entitled to a pension. He became something of a celebrity when the "Sunday Post' interviewed him.

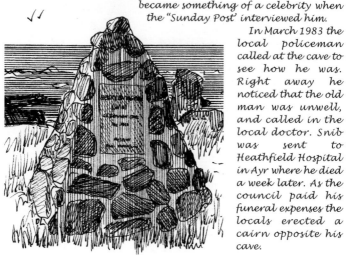

In March 1983 the local policeman called at the cave to see how he was. Right away he noticed that the old man was unwell, and called in the local doctor. Snib was sent to Heathfield Hospital in Ayr where he died a week later. As the council paid his funeral expenses the locals erected a cairn opposite his cave.

South of Bennane Head is a two mile stretch of shingly beach, extending to Ballantrae.

In October 1926 the "Richard" ran aground on the beach north of Ballantrae during a heavy gale. The three-masted schooner had been built in the USA and was only four years old at the time. It was owned and manned by a Danish crew from Thuro. The wreck survived on the shore for a number of years.

Part of the raised beach north of Ballantrae was used as an 18-hole golf course, but this has long-since closed, and the land returned to agriculture.

Just before reaching Ballantrae's Park End one becomes aware of the round tower on top of the former cliff of the raised beach. This was an old windmill, and the eminence is known as Mill Hill. The windmill dates from the 18th century and is a well-preserved example of the "vaulted tower" type. It can be reached by following a pathway from Ballantrae.

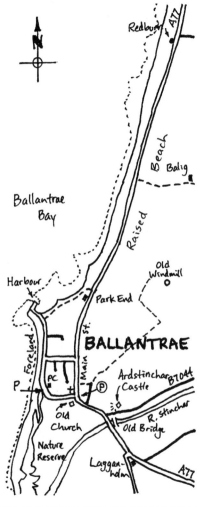

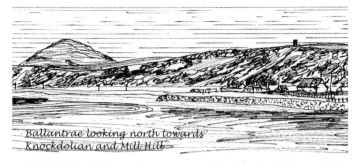

Ballantrae looking north towards Knockdolian and Mill Hill

Ballantrae, a picturesque former fishing port, is the last village before Galloway. It was only established in 1617 when an Act of Parliament allowed the removal of the church to the present site. Previously the centre of the parish was located at Kirkcudbright Innertig, 2½ miles inland.

The main street runs on a north-south axis, turning left sharply at the southern end, heading for the bridge over the River Stinchar. At the road junction is the Parish Church of 1819. This is a fairly plain building, distinguished only by its windows and small spirelet, added in 1891, on which is a clock. The church is open on most days in the summer, and within can be seen memorials to Lord Ballantrae and David MacGibbon (1831-1902), architect and co-author of one of the classic guides to Scotland's castles. From 1826-30 the minister was Rev. Thomas Burns, a nephew of the bard, Robert Burns.

The King's Arms Hotel in the village was erected in 1770 as one of the main coaching inns on the main road south. Locals claim that the stone used in its construction was taken from Ardstinchar Castle. There are some older buildings - the Manse (1736) and former schoolmaster's house (1750).

In January 1876 Robert Louis Stevenson spent a night at Ballantrae and liked the name so much that he used it in the title of his "Master of Ballantrae", although the novel was actually set in Galloway. The locals were not too impressed by RLS - they were so disturbed by his flamboyant clothing that they threw stones at him!

Ballantrae harbour is little more than a tiny pier, built on the headland of Rock Nays. The basin was excavated from the solid rock and the pier constructed at a total cost of £6,000. Nevertheless, the harbour was at one time an important fishery, for here in 1890 there were cured 1,322 barrels of white herrings annually, landed by 516 boats. The total workforce included 921 fishermen, 78 fish curers, 51 coopers and 800 others at that time!

Sheds at Ballantrae harbour

The pier is L-shaped in plan, the seaward part protected by a wall above the level of the roadway. On the inner face, steps drop down into the water. Along the foreshore are a few timber and rubble gear sheds. The row of fourteen single-storey plus attic cottages were originally occupied by fishermen.

Steamers making their way from Glasgow to Stranraer and back previously used the pier at Ballantrae, but those halcyon days are long gone. Today it is home to a few pleasure craft and lobster fishermen. Lobster creels can often be seen lying on barrows at the harbour side.

The registration letters "BA" represent Ballantrae and can be seen on various boats in Carrick ports and beyond. The only other Ayrshire registration is "AR" for Ayr, but this is much less common.

Ayrshire Coast-Bargany Aisle

In the old graveyard can be seen the Bargany mausoleum, burial place of the Kennedys of Bargany. An inscription details its significance:

> This aisle contains the burial-place of the family of Bargany and Ardstinchar, chief of the name of Kennedy, and a monument raised over the remains of Gilbert, the XVIth Baron, who was slain in a feudal conflict with his cousin, the Earl of Cassillis, at Maybole in 1601, at the early age of 25, at which conflict, when overpowered by numbers, Bargany displayed the most consummate bravery.

Bargany Aisle

The feud was over which branch had superiority over the other, and lasted for forty years. Sir Walter Scott used the facts to write "Auchindrane - An Ayrshire Tragedy" and S.R. Crockett based much of "The Grey Man" on it.

Gilbert Kennedy had tried to kill the 5th Earl of Cassillis in an ambush in the winter of 1601. He failed, and a few days later, on 11 December, Cassillis and his men came upon Gilbert at a spot known as Lady Corse, north of Maybole. A short battle ensued, but Gilbert was struck from behind and seriously wounded. He was later taken to Ayr where he died.

The memorial in the aisle comprises of an elaborate tomb, within which are representations of Gilbert and his wife, Janet Stewart, who had been one of the Queen's "maideynes". One thousand mourners brought the corpse of Gilbert from Ayr to Ballantrae.

134

Ardstinchar Castle

On a low rocky ridge of Mains Hill stands the ruined tower of Ardstinchar Castle. The ruin is easily accessible from the main road, but the walls are dangerous. The castle affords views over the village and foot of the Stinchar.

The castle was probably built around 1450 for Hugh Kennedy, of the Bargany branch. He was originally destined for the priesthood, being a second son, but he gave this up and travelled to the continent where he became a close friend of Charles VII of France. He went with the king to the Holy Land, and received from him "gritt rewairdis of gold and mony", with which he was able to buy Ardstinchar lands (for £10) and build the castle.

It is recorded that Mary Queen of Scots spent a night at the castle on 8th August 1566 whilst on a pilgrimage. During the Kennedy feud, the Cassillis branch threatened to blow it up, but was persuaded against this. In 1650 ownership passed to Sir John Hamilton.

Ardstinchar had three vaults, each over the other, and it has been speculated that this is the reason why the tower has collapsed, leaving only one corner complete to the wallhead. Indeed, in 1696, William Abercrummie noted that the tower was "mostly now ruined", so the castle cannot have had a very long life. To the west of the tower is a large triangular courtyard, the walls of which have long-since gone, but which can be made out on the ground.

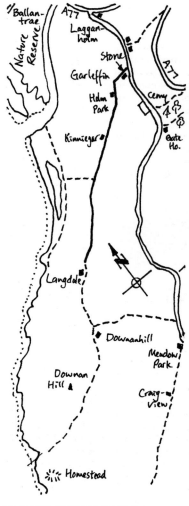

From Ardstinchar the new bridge of 1964 crosses the River Stinchar. This replaces the old bridge of 1770, which is now closed even to pedestrians due to the crumbling masonry. It has parapet copes joined with mortise and tenons, and three arches, one smaller than the rest, perhaps indicating that it once served a mill lade. Stinchar Cottage at the north end may have once been a toll house.

At Lagganholm the main A77 should be avoided by cyclists and pedestrians by following a minor road towards Garleffin. This was originally the main road south, crossing over by Ballochdowan and Finnarts Hill before dropping into Glen App.

At Garleffin one can see a standing stone located in the front garden of one of the cottages. There were formerly eight of these, but they were removed from the field to enhance its agricultural yield. In 1829 Ludovic MacLellan Mann calculated that, from their alignment, the stones recorded a solar eclipse that took place at noon, 31 December 2709 BC!

From Garleffin the pedestrian can follow the old road south to Finnarts Bay, at the foot of Glen App. The road passes the cemetery and crosses the Colling Bridge before climbing Knockenfinnick hill and passing Meadow Park and Craigalbert farms. At Currarie Cottage a left turn should be taken, crossing a low ridge before dropping to Low Ballochdowan. Here a surfaced public road can be followed east for half a mile to Killantringan Bridge (the cottage has a pottery and craft shop) before striking west once more. Alternatively, farm tracks can be taken past the site of Balminnoch and Shallochwreck to Craigans, where the surfaced road from Killantringan is picked up once more.

From Craigans the road is followed towards Glendrisaig farm, after which it degenerates into a track over the shoulder of Knockcriest and through the gap to Finnarts farm.

Below Knockchriest a zigzag track can be followed down to the tiny bay called Portandea, where the Two-door Cove is a distinctive rock feature.

Almost at the highest point of the pass are two standing stones a few yards to the west of the road, relics from the Bronze Age.

The original roadway dropped alongside Aultygunnoch Burn to Finnarts farm, but this road is no longer visible on the ground. Instead a track strikes down the slopes at a lesser angle towards Craiganlea House (in reality, just a cottage!). The A77 is only half a mile beyond, across the Bridge of the Mark. Alternatively, a track can be followed back past Finnarts farm to the bay at the foot of the Water of App.

Homestead

Wilson's Glen

N

Dove Cove

Knock Gowan

Donald Bowie

Currarie Glen

Path to Craigans

Currarie Port

Craigangal

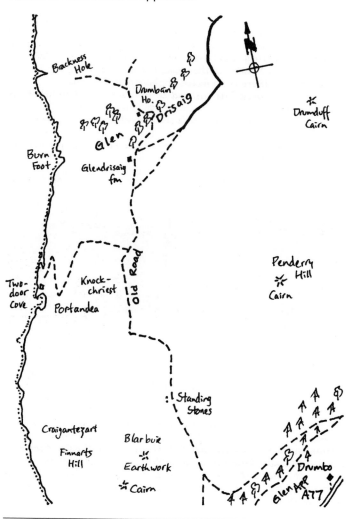

Brackness Hole

Drumbain Ho.

Glen Drisaig

Drumduff Cairn

Burn Foot

Glendrisaig fm

Penderry Hill Cairn

Two-door Cove

Knock-chriest

Old Road

Portandea

Craigantezart

Finnarts Hill

Blarbuie

Earthwork

Cairn

Standing Stones

Glenapp

Drumbo

A77

The driver has to leave the coast behind from Ballantrae to Finnarts Bay, for there is no place on which to put a modern road on this rugged stretch of countryside. The minor road from Garleffin past Craigalbert and Low Ballochdowan can be taken to keep as close as possible to the coast, but as the sea is quite distant from the road there is no feeling of being at the coast.

The motorist has instead to follow the A77 uphill from Ballantrae Bridge, past the wooded policies of Glenapp Castle (1870, David Bryce) to a small settlement of modern houses at Smyrton. The road levels off once more, passing through woods to the open moorland. This area is often subject to drifting snow in the winter months. To the west of the road, in

Glenapp Castle

the middle of the moss, can be seen a memorial to Robert Cunningham killed in a blizzard here in 1928.

The road drops quickly into Glen App, passing the entrance to Carlock House, seat of Lord Inchcape. The glen is virtually straight, a great natural fissure formed by the Southern Upland fault. Half way down the glen is the small Glenapp Church, erected in 1850 as a chapel of ease and restored in 1910 by P. MacGregor Chalmers. Here is a large memorial stone commemorating the 1st Earl of Inchcape, as well as a memorial to Elsie Mackay, killed in an aeroplane accident in 1928.

It is not until Finnarts Bay is reached that the main road returns to the coast, but at this point there is only one mile of Ayrshire left!

Ayrshire Coast-Postman's Memorial

The cross in the middle of Ballochdowan Moor was erected "In memory of Robert Cunningham, postman, who perished here in a snowstorm, 28th December 1908". It was paid for by public

subscription and with funds raised by the Postmens' Federation. Cunningham lived in Ballantrae's Main Street, opposite the Stinchar Lodge Hotel, wherein his fiancée was the daughter of the innkeeper. He was 27 in 1908, and a much-loved postman in the local area. That winter was long and hard, and the snow so heavy that the mail could not be delivered on several occasions. The December blizzard had howled for three days, and the snow was so deep that it lay right down to the edge of the sea - a very rare occurrence.

After a few days Cunningham decided that he might be able to deliver the mail. The going was tough, but he managed to walk all the way down Glen App to Finnarts. On his

return journey he delivered a letter to the gamekeeper on Carlock estate, who realised that Cunningham was struggling and invited him to spend the night there. But the intrepid postman refused, as he was keen to get home to his fiancée. Tragically, he never made it back to the village.

A search for Cunningham took days, and it was his brother who eventually found the corpse. It seems he had stumbled and knocked his head on a post, after which he died of exposure. His fiancée, her heart broken, was never to marry.

At Finnarts farm there used to be a small mansion known as Finnarts House, but this has long-since disappeared. Still existing, however, is the cylindrical doocot on the hillside above where the house stood. The roadway can be followed west from Finnarts through the Garry Wood to an old hump-backed bridge across the Water of App.

Finnarts Bay is located at the foot of the water. The beach is stony, but it is very popular with sea-anglers. The north end of the bay is protected by Garry Point, where a cave can be found among the rocks. Prominent on a rock buff on Garry Hill is a former lookout tower, erected during the war. A fish farm is located in the bay.

The south side of the bay is known as Port Sally. Here can be seen the remains of a Second World War gunnery emplacement.

Old gun emplacement

Various ruins of brick and concrete gun houses are visible amongst the bracken and brambles, guarding the entrance to Loch Ryan.

Loch Ryan was a strategic centre during the Second World War. Many of the Mulberry Harbours used in the Normandy landing in June 1944 were built here. This all took place on the Wigtownshire side of the border, and is therefore beyond the scope of this book.

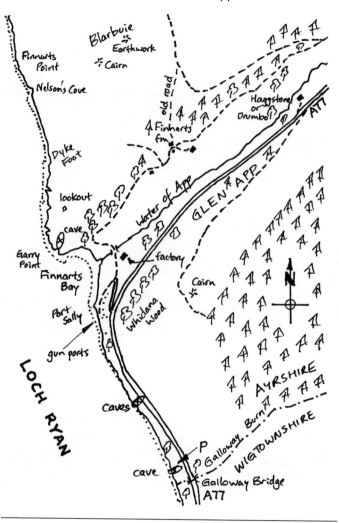

Finnarts Bay looking towards Garry Point
and the lookout tower

From Finnarts Bay the A77 is followed for just half a mile or so
southward to the Galloway Bridge, after which one leaves Ayrshire
and enters Wigtownshire. Here also one leaves the ancient
kingdom of Carrick and enters Galloway. A parking area is
located by the roadside just north of the boundary.

The small stream that drops from Laight Moor is known as
the Galloway Burn, and it forms the boundary hereabouts. A
small waterfall is visible from the road. The cottage on the
Galloway side of the bridge is known as Marchburn, again
indicating that two distinct areas of land are divided here.

The coast of Loch Ryan has a few small caves to either side
of the border, two of which are known as the Black and White
caves.

The Galloway Burn marks a major boundary in south west
Scotland, one that has been delineated for centuries. Formerly the
kingdoms of Galloway and Carrick were separated by this little
stream, and even today the authorities of South Ayrshire and
Dumfries & Galloway use it to mark their borders. Wigtownshire to
the south is like a different country - the locals seem to talk in a
different way, and the landscape gradually takes on a new
appearance. To follow the Wigtownshire coast is a whole new
adventure.

Ayrshire Coast-Bibliography

In addition to the following books, the author has referred to numerous guidebooks and brochures produced by various historical groups, tourist boards, visitor centres, etc.

Alexander, A.S., "Across Watersheds", Robert Maclehose, Glasgow, 1939.

Andrew, Ken, "Kyle and Carrick District", Alloway Publishing, Ayr, 1981.

Boyle, Andrew, "The Ayrshire Book of Burns Lore", Alloway Publishing, Darvel, 1985.

Campbell, JRD, "Largs Through the Centuries", Largs & District History Society, 1995.

Close, Rob, "Ayrshire & Arran", RIAS, Edinburgh, 1992.

Cuthbertson, D.C., "Carrick Days", Grant & Murray, Edinburgh, 1933.

Czerkawska, Catherine Lucy, "Fisherfolk of Carrick", Molendinar Press, Glasgow, 1975.

Davis, Michael, "The Castles and Mansions of Ayrshire", privately published, 1991.

Lawson, Rev. Roderick, "Ailsa Craig", J & R Parlane, Paisley, 1888.

    "Places of Interest about Girvan", J & R Parlane, Paisley, 1892.

Love, Dane, "Pictorial History of Ayr", Alloway Publishing, Darvel, 1995.

    "Ayr Stories", Fort Publishing, Ayr, 2000.

MacGibbon, David, & Ross, Thomas, "The Castellated and Domestic Architecture of Scotland", David Douglas, Edinburgh, 1887-92.

Moir, Peter & Crawford, Ian, "Clyde Shipwrecks", Moir Crawford, Wemyss Bay, 1988.

"New Statistical Account of Scotland" (Ayrshire), William Blackwood, Edinburgh, 1842.

"Ordnance Gazetteer of Scotland", London, nd.

Steele, John & Noreen, "Whispers of Horse Island", Argyll, Publishing, Glendaruel, 1999.

Strawhorn, John, "The History of Irvine", John Donald, Edinburgh, 1985.

    "The History of Ayr", John Donald, Edinburgh, 1989.

    "The History of Prestwick", John Donald, Edinburgh, 1994.

Strawhorn, John, & Andrew, Ken, "Discovering Ayrshire", John Donald, Edinburgh, 1988.

Tranter, Nigel, "The Fortified House in Scotland Vol. III - South West Scotland", Oliver & Boyd, Edinburgh, 1962.

Wilkins, Frances, "Strathclyde's Smuggling Story", Wyre Forest Press, Kidderminster, 1992.